$45-

MILITARY
HARLEY-DAVIDSON

MILITARY
HARLEY-DAVIDSON

Pat Ware

Ian Allan
PUBLISHING

This book could not have been produced without the assistance of the following people:

Martin Baldessari for picture research at The National Archives, Washington DC (NA): Fred Crismon (FC) and David Doyle (DD); Luther Hanson at the US Army Quartermasters Museum, Fort Lee, VA (USQM); Richard Hill and Gerald Prinsloo at the South African National Museum of Military History (SANMMH); Debbie Brentnell at the National Archives of Canada (NAC); David Arenson (DA): Paul Turner at DK Images, London (DK); Andrew Renwick at the Royal Air Force Museum (RAFM); Zach Vowell at the University of Texas for access to the Robert Runyon Collection (RR/UTX); National Archives of Australia (NAA). Also to Doreen Cadwalader (DC); the Ministry of Defence/Crown Copyright (MoD). Finally to Darrell McCalla at the Barber Vintage Motorcycle Museum, Birmingham, Alabama (DC/BVMM) also to Phil Royal (PR); John Blackman (JBn) and Simon Thomson (ST) for their superb colour images.

Jasper Spencer-Smith,
Bournemouth, England,
October 2007.

Conceived & edited:
Jasper Spencer-Smith

Text design and layout:
Crispin Goodall Design

InDesign editor: Jennie Murray

Jacket design: Ian Allan studio

Scanning:
JPS Limited, Branksome Poole,
BH21 1DJ, England

Produced:
JSS Publishing Ltd
P.O. Box 6031, Bournemouth,
BH1 9AT, England

First published 2007

ISBN 0 7110 3191 6
ISBN 978 0 7110 3191 3

Published by Ian Allan Publishing

An imprint of Ian Allan Publishing Ltd, Hersham, Surrey KT12 4RG Printed by Ian Allan Publishing Ltd, Hersham Surrey KT12 4RG

Code 0711/C

visit the Ian Allan Publishing web site at:
www.ianallanpublishing.com

Above: Members of the Los Angeles motorcycle club attend a rally at Venice, California in 1910. (NA)

Title spread: A US Army 76mm GMC (gun motor carriage) M10 passes through the town of Percy in Normandy, France, July 1944. The M10 in British service was known as the Wolverine. The Harley-Davidson WA is the mount of the MP directing traffic. (NA)

Contents page: Japanese police officers on patrol in a licence-built Harley-Davidson combination, c1920.

CONTENTS

INTRODUCTION

Spoken in the same sentence, the words 'Harley-Davidson' and 'military motorcycle' generally conjure up images of the iconic Model WLA, the big 737cc (45cu.in) V-twin machine, purposefully devoid of chrome and ornament, and equipped with tan leather panniers and a rifle sleeve. The company built some 78,000 examples of the WLA during World War Two and, in Europe, it earned the name of the 'Liberator'. But, as is so often the case, scratch beneath the surface and there is a lot more to it than this. The WLA was not the only military Harley-Davidson and, even during World War Two, examples of the Models E and U were supplied to the military. We certainly should not forget the very BMW-like Model XA, more than 1,000 examples of which were constructed for possible use in the deserts of North Africa.

Back in World War One, motorcycles were seen as the logical replacement for the horse. Period photographs show motorcyclists struggling across the cratered ground of the front lines on primitive 'bone-shaker' machines, or speeding between command centres on dusty roads, carrying messages which, in subsequent conflicts, would be transmitted by radio. Motorcycles were also used for reconnaissance, as well as being pressed into service as stretcher carriers, machine-gun mounts, and ammunition carriers.

Motorcycles were there from the beginning, playing a vital role in the mechanisation of warfare.

And, almost as old as the industry itself, the Harley-Davidson Motor Company built its first motorcycle in 1903, starting to supply machines for military use less than a decade later. Huge numbers were purchased by the US government for use during World War One, and the first US soldier into Germany, at the end of that terrible conflict, was said to be riding a Harley-Davidson.

Between the wars, there were experiments with armoured motorcycles and, in the earliest days of World War Two, the military motorcycle still seemed the logical choice for a myriad of roles, including the mechanisation of shock troops. Germany, particularly, favoured mounting infantry on big motorcycle sidecar outfits, which carried machine guns or mortar launchers, for their *Blitzkrieg* style of warfare. A regular *Wehrmacht* infantry division on the Eastern Front in the early stage of World War Two was equipped with an average of 452 motorcycle outfits.

Right: Photographed in August 1950, this white-painted WLA belongs to Sergeant Ralph Campbell of Company B, 709th Miliatry Police Battalion. Campbell was the first military policeman in Europe to be equipped with two-way radio on his motorcycle.(NA)

Britain and the USA considered going down the same route. Training photographs show intrepid motorcycle-mounted US Cavalrymen posing astride their mechanical horses, carbines at the ready, or throwing their machines down and crouching behind them in a firing position, the motorcycle providing a degree of cover and a steady support for a gun.

But, for all this, the Allies never did use the motorcycle in combat (only for messenger duties) and it was almost certainly the entry of the Jeep in service that changed everything.

Above: The 1915 V-twin Model F was fitted with the new three-speed transmission and a mechanical oil pump; there were also technical changes to the engine. These features provided better performance and enhanced reliability. (DK)

Above right: Deliveries of the 737cc (45cu. in.) side-valve twin engined WLA started in 1939 and continued into the 1950s. The bike was efffectively a militarised Model WL, which had first appeared in 1937. (USQM)

The combination of lightweight, four wheels and all-wheel drive made the Jeep far more versatile than either a solo motorcycle or a sidecar outfit and with a carrying capacity of 336lb (250kg), it was also better suited to mounting a machine gun or even a light anti-tank gun. The Jeep was equally capable of being used as a stretcher carrier, communications vehicle or convoy escort. And, in truth, a Jeep could go almost cover the same terrain that a motorcycle could and, at the same time, could carry more men or cargo, in somewhat greater comfort.

At the instigation of the US War Department, Harley-Davidson experimented with shaft drive, like the big BMW and Zündapp outfits used by the *Wehrmacht*. The company also built a prototype three wheel (two driving) field car using the 'Servi-Car' as a basis. But by the middle of World War Two, motorcycles had been mostly relegated to a behind-the-lines role, used mainly by Military Police units, naval shore patrols and convoy escorts.

Nevertheless, the Harley-Davidson Motor Company supplied some 88,000 motorcycles during the war, the

Left: Members of the 1st Division US First Army use a shell-torn barn as a temporary motor pool. The date is February 1945, the motorcycle is the ubiquitous WLA.(NA)

majority of which were the iconic Model WLA. Production of military machines reduce dramatically after 1945 and the US Army virtually abandoned the motorcycle during the 1950s. The same was less true of Europe but, with two notable exceptions, the smaller domestically-produced models were generally favoured over the big Harley-Davidson.

It was not until the late 1970s that military authorities started to look seriously at motorcycles again, but by this time the Japanese 'invasion' into the marketplace had decimated the world's motorcycle manufacturers. Harley-Davidson remained in the market by buying the manufacturing rights to an Italian-derived, British-designed Armstrong/CCM, trailbike the MT500 and MT350 which they supplied to Britain, Jordan and Canada. Despite the company's best efforts, the US Army chose to buy Kawasaki.

By the turn of the 20th century, the military Harley-Davidson was a thing of the past, most of its roles taken over by versatile 4x4 vehicles.

Since the dark days of the early 1980s, the Harley-Davidson Motor Company has gone from strength to strength, with lifestyle products that appeal to all motorcycling 'outlaws' no matter how respectable and law-abiding. The glory days of the military motorcycle are gone.

Whilst it is true that the Model XA and the British-designed Armstrong MT (for which Harley-Davidson purchased the manufacturing rights in 1987) were the company's only purpose-built military machines, Harley-Davidson's 100-year history virtually parallels the 100-year history of the military motorcycle. So, not surprisingly, many of the company's products designed for civilians have found service with the military.

This book is an effort to gather together in one volume the story of the Harley-Davidson military motorcycle before it is lost for ever not just the pure military Model WLA and XA, but all of the company's products, which have either been used in service or trialled by the armies of many countries around the world.

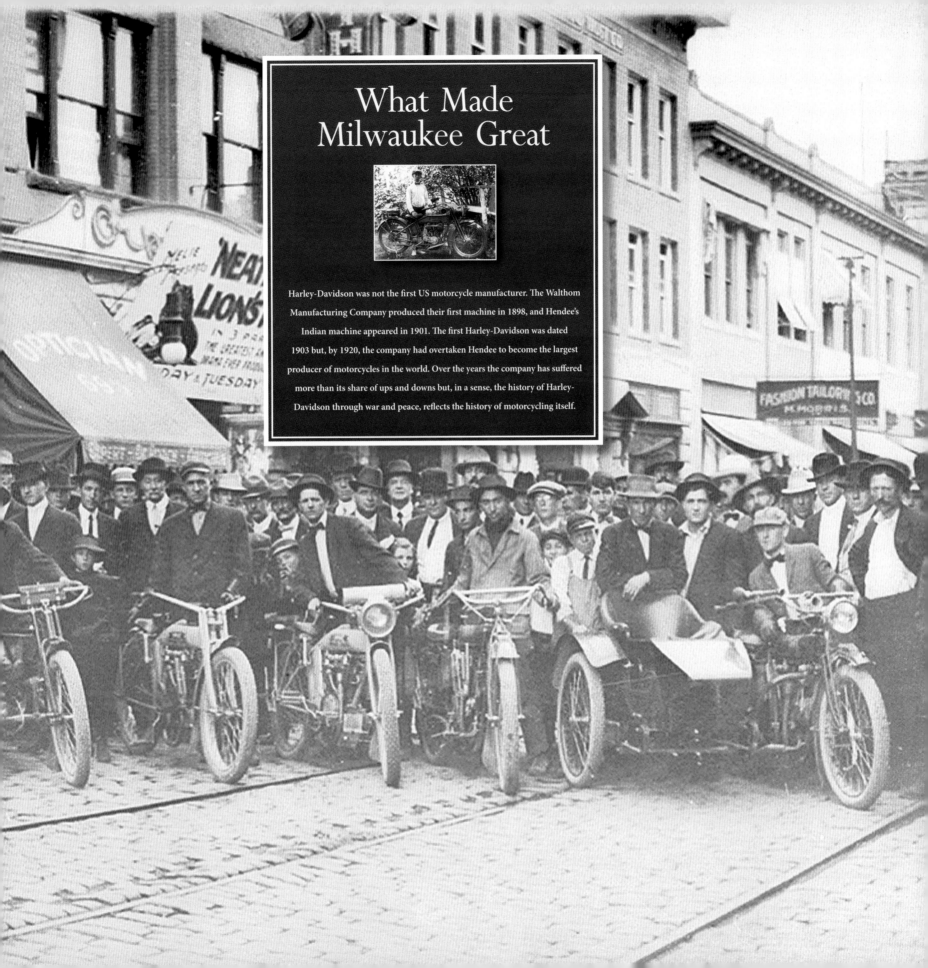

What Made Milwaukee Great

Harley-Davidson was not the first US motorcycle manufacturer. The Walthom Manufacturing Company produced their first machine in 1898, and Hendee's Indian machine appeared in 1901. The first Harley-Davidson was dated 1903 but, by 1920, the company had overtaken Hendee to become the largest producer of motorcycles in the world. Over the years the company has suffered more than its share of ups and downs but, in a sense, the history of Harley-Davidson through war and peace, reflects the history of motorcycling itself.

CHAPTER 1 WHAT MADE MILWAUKEE GREAT

The name Harley-Davidson has become synonymous with the American motorcycle and yet, at one time, the USA was home to some 325 motorcycle manufacturers. From small beginnings, the company quickly grew to become not only the largest producer of motorcycles in the USA but, for a period, was also the largest producer of such machines in the world.

William S. Harley and Arthur Davidson founded what became the Harley-Davidson Motor Company in 1901. Within 20 years, Harley-Davidson had become the world's largest motorcycle manufacturer, and today, despite facing near ruin in the 1980s, remains the only volume motorcycle manufacturer in the USA. In its 100-year history, Harley-Davidson has become an iconic brand, representing an independent lifestyle which is embraced by hundreds of thousands sold across the globe and recognised by many, many more.

Yet, alongside this charismatic image, the company has also produced an enormous number of ordinary motorcycles, none more typical than those used by military and law-enforcement agencies. Harley-Davidson supplied its first military motorcycle in 1912, furnished the US Army with thousands of solo and sidecar outfits during World War One, and will forever be associated with the iconic WLA of World War Two a motorcycle apparently dubbed the 'Liberator' by the grateful people of France, Belgium and the Netherlands who were liberated as the Allied armies swept across Europe after 1944. And if motorcycles are no longer widely used by

the world's armies, this is certainly not the fault of Harley-Davidson whose products could always be relied on.

The company grew from humble beginnings. William Harley and Arthur Davidson had been school-friends in Milwaukee since the early 1890s and, although both had been born in the USA, Harley's working-class parents had emigrated from England (possibly from the Manchester area) and the Davidsons were of Scottish origin.

After leaving school, the young men (one year apart in age) found employment in various engineering shops in the Milwaukee area. Both were interested in the new-fangled motorcycles and, in their spare time, worked on a small DeDion-type engine of around 115cc (7cu.in) capacity. At first, they were frustrated by the lack of suitable workshop premises, and it was not until 1903 that Harley was allowed the use of a small, modestly-equipped machine shop. In the spring of 1903, by now also assisted by Walter Davidson (brother of Arthur), the engine was finally completed and was fitted into a heavy-duty pedal-cycle frame. Sadly, the flimsy tubing that was adequate for the stresses of a pedal cycle proved unequal to the loads imposed by the engine. By the

Right: It was not long before police forces in the USA began to see the advantage of motorcycles. Dating from 1908, this single-cylinder model, belonging to the Detroit Police Department, features a fork-mounted speedometer. (DA)

Previous pages: Members of the Butte Motorcycle Club, Montana attend a rally in the town's main street, 1914. (NA)

Above: By 1913, Harley-Davidson had established more than 200 dealers across the USA and motorcycling became very popular. This single-cylinder machine of around 1913 features magneto ignition and is still fitted with the distinctive 'bicycle pedals'. (DA)

autumn of that year, Harley and the two Davidson brothers had turned their attention to producing a more powerful engine, basing the design on drawings which they had acquired from Emil Kroeger, reputedly a workmate.

The second engine was also a single-cylinder type, this time with a capacity of 455cc (27.75cu.in). When installed in the cycle frame, drive to the rear wheel was by means of a flat leather belt, with pedal assistance to get the machine moving from a standing start; the 'clutch', such as it was, took the form of a spring-loaded device, which applied tension to the belt, using the resulting slippage to provide progressive drive to the rear wheel. The machine ran well but the lightweight cycle frame was still not strong enough and it became obvious that a purpose-built frame would be required, designed from the outset to absorb the increased loads of a motorised machine.

A brazed heavy-duty tubular frame was produced which mounted a rectangular-shaped fuel tank beneath the top tube and carried the engine ahead of the pedal bracket,

Right: The simple heavy-duty leather belt drive used on the X-8 Harley-Davidson. (DK)

Below: By 1912, when this 494cc (30cu.in) X-8 single-cylinder machine appeared, Harley-Davidsons had acquired the nickname 'The Silent Gray Fellow'. Although it featured a number of improvements, it was clearly a direct development of the original 1905 machine. (DK)

17

Above: From 1917, as this Model J demonstrates, Harley-Davidson started to offer motorcycles equipped with sidecars. Not only did this allow riders to be accompanied by a passenger but it also opened up new markets, including package delivery. (DA)

supported by a single frame loop. The front forks were not sprung but were made from extra-heavy tubing and were supported in large bearings. The machine was still fitted with pedals, but the wheel rims were wider than those used on the cycle, and consequently the tyres were of larger section, also more powerful brakes were fitted. The new machine was capable of 25mph (40kph). Following a period of testing, both men believed that the machine was ready to offer for sale to the public. Members of the public had already seen the motorcycle in use, gaining the partners a small backlog of serious enquiries. One machine, as yet un-built, had already

been sold to Henry Meyer, a school-friend of the partners. Davidson's father, also named William, a carpenter by trade, erected a 150sq.ft (14sq.m) single-storey wooden shed at the bottom of the garden of the family home. The location was at the intersection of 38th Street and Highland Avenue, Milwaukee. With the legend 'Harley-Davidson Motor Co' painted on the front door, the new company was open for business.

Above: Highly-decorated company delivery vehicle prepared for an Independence Day parade in Milwaukee. The machine is a Model F. (DA)

William Harley enrolled at the Engineering Department of the University of Wisconsin to learn more about his chosen subject, waiting on tables in the evenings to support himself. Arthur Davidson started to assemble the motorcycles. Two machines were built during the winter of 1903 and 1904 and, during this time, Davidson continued with his day job and relied on assistance from part-time workers. In the spring of 1904, his brother Walter joined the firm fulltime, and four employees were taken on. The size of the shed was doubled to 300sq.ft (28sq.m). The first dealer, C. H. Lang of Chicago, Illinois was appointed.

By 1905, the company had built and sold 10 examples of what was being described as the Model 1, but was restrained by a lack of space and working capital. Salvation appeared in the form of the Davidson's uncle, James McLay, who loaned sufficient money to enable the company to purchase land and build premises, now measuring a massive 2240sq.ft (208sq.m). This was located at the junction of 27th and

Above: The twin-cylinder Model J appeared in 1915 and was a considerable step forward. The three-speed gearbox, mechanical oil pump and electric lighting made this machine faster and more reliable. The Model F was similar but lacked electric lighting. (DA)

Chestnut Street, Milwaukee – the latter subsequently to be renamed Juneau Avenue. In 1906 there were six employees and sales totalled 50 machines of what was now the Model 2. The change indicating the fitting of primitive front suspension. In 1907, the Model 3 was introduced and sales figures increased to 150. The following year, there were now 35 employees, and the company sold 450 of the Model 4. On 17 September 1907, the company was incorporated as the Harley-Davidson Motor Company, with the stock split between the four founders. Walter Davidson was named as

President and General Manager. The eldest of the Davidson brothers, William A. Davidson, then 36, gave up his job with the Milwaukee Road railway to become Vice-President and Works Manager. Arthur Davidson finally quit his day job as a pattern maker and was named Secretary and Sales Manager, devoting his energies to sales promotion.

Although still at the university William S. Harley was Treasurer, Chief Engineer and Designer.

The first police motorcycle was supplied, in 1908, to the Detroit Police Department. While the following year saw two further, and very significant, 'firsts' for the long-term development of the company. Curiously, this was the first year in which spare parts were made available. Perhaps of greater long-term importance to the development of the marque, 1909 saw the first appearance of the V-twin engine, a design with which the company has been identified up to the present day. The engine appeared on the Model 5-D in 1909 although it had already been prototyped and shown to the public at the 1907 Chicago Motor Show. With an angle of 45° between the cylinders, the engine, which was of F-head design (overhead inlet and side exhaust valves), produced around 7bhp from a capacity of 880cc (53.7cu.in). The inlet valves, located in the head, were of the automatic type which means that they were simply sucked open by the descending piston, whilst the exhaust valves were integral with the one-piece cylinder casting. The engine proved troublesome and the Model 5-D could scarcely have been considered a runaway success, with just 27 examples built in the first year, and just one 5-D the following year. By 1911, the unreliable automatic valves had been replaced by conventional camshaft operation.

In 1912, the Model X-8-D appeared fitted with chain drive, which meant that a mechanical clutch was required. With this change in place, the new V-twin proved to be more than reliable, and Harley-Davidson motorcycles were at last firmly on the road to success.

With a regular workforce of 1,076 employees, the company ordered the construction of a six-storey building totalling 187,750sq.ft (17,442sq.m). More than 3,800 motorcycles were constructed during 1912, and there were now around 200 Harley-Davidson dealers nationwide. A dedicated spare parts department was also created.

The US Army first purchased motorcycles as early as 1913 and, although three US manufacturers predominated at this time – Indian, (made by the Hendee Manufacturing Company) Excelsior and Harley-Davidson – the government's first such purchases were almost certainly of Indian 'Powerplus' machines. However, Harley-Davidson had already secured its first military order a year earlier when company minutes for 1912 noted that a number of motorcycles – probably Model X-8-A civilian machines fitted with a 492cc (30cu.in) single-cylinder engine – had been supplied to the Japanese Imperial Army for evaluation 'without spares'.

The year 1915 saw the company discontinue the use of the two-speed rear hub on V-twin machines, replacing it with a three-speed sliding-gear transmission, on which the final and primary drive chains were located on the left-hand side of the engine. This was the last year in which the models were consecutively numbered, the Model 11 of 1915 giving way to the Model 16 the following year. From then on numbering by date became the norm.

By 1916, the US Army had also started to purchase Harley-Davidson motorcycles.

On 16 March 1916, the US government ordered an initial quantity of a dozen of the Model 16-J with a 999cc (61cu.in) V-twin inlet-over-exhaust power unit, coupled to a three-speed transmission. The civilian price was $310 but presumably the government did not expect to simply pay the 'list' price. Company records show that a number of sidecars were also supplied to the US Army, alongside the standard single-passenger sidecar, there were also three types of special sidecar: purpose-made for carrying ammunition (code AC), stretchers (SC), and for tripod-mounted machine gun (GC). The latter type was designed by William Harley. The first motorcycles were delivered to the Mexican border area within two days, and were used by forces pursuing Doroteo Aranga's troops - although he was better known under his adopted name of Francisco 'Pancho' Villa - into Mexico. Legend has it that Villa's men were mounted on Indian motorcycles!

A week or so later, the US government ordered a further six Harley-Davidsons.

World War One

When the US entered World War One in 1917 motorcycles were widely used to mechanise the expeditionary force. Harley-Davidson Models J and F were supplied to all of the Allied armies and were typically used by dispatch riders, military police in traffic control, medical teams, wiring

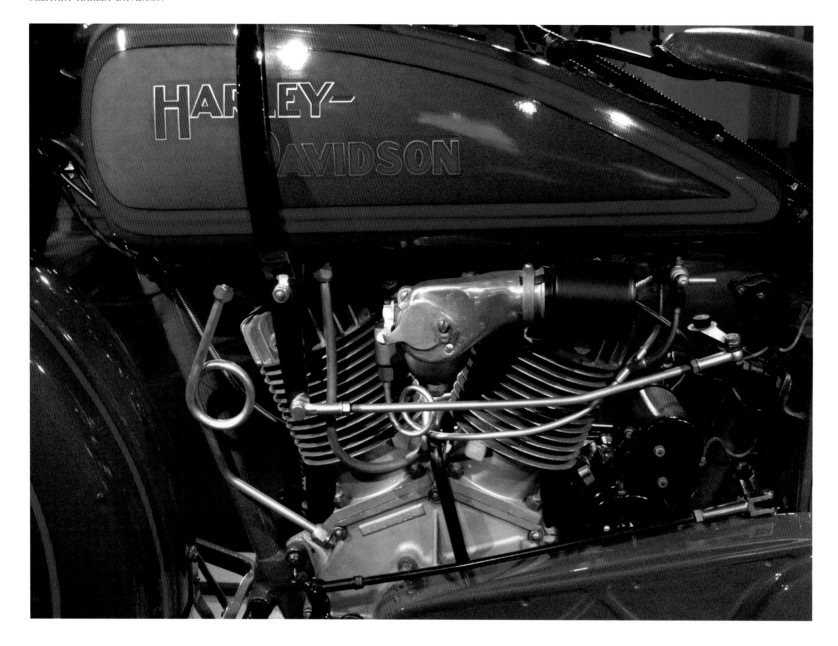

parties, and for escort duties. True, the original grey paint had given way to a more military olive green finish, but these were otherwise standard civilian machines. It was not long before half of the company's output was being supplied to the government and, by the end of the conflict, between 12 and 18,000 Harley-Davidson motorcycles had been delivered to the US Army. Clearly this had some effect on civilian sales but, nevertheless, for all but the last six months of the war, Harley-Davidsons remained available to civilian customers.

The inter-war years

Around two-thirds of the machines which had been supplied to the US government remained in the USA. At the end of the war there was an abundance of surplus motorcycles, many of which were showing an extremely low mileage. Whilst this could have had serious repercussions on sales of new machines, there was, on the other hand, an increase in consumer awareness of motorcycles as a result of their widespread use in France and Belgium. Harley-Davidson, unlike Indian (who had neglected civilian sales between

Above: Fitted with acetylene lighting equipment, these are clearly Model F sidecar models; note the calcium-carbide container behind the handlebars. The sidecars were designated, LC - passenger carrier; AC - ammunition carrier; GC - maching gun carrier and SC-stretcher carrier. (RR/UTX)

Left: The twin-cylinder Model J appeared in 1922 and was a considerable step forward. The three-speed gearbox, mechanical oil pump and electric lighting made this machine faster and more reliable. (DK)

1917 and 1918), had continued to build their dealer network during the war years.

All of this meant that the company was in a very strong position, and peacetime production quickly resumed. Sales for 1918 reached 26,708, including 8,095 examples of the Presto-Lite equipped Model FUS for government use. Sales for 1919 were similarly successful with a very creditable 23,279 units, of which 7,521 were of the government Model FUS. It is not clear whether these were intended for the military or whether they were also intended for use by other

Right: Military Model J with standard factory sidecar. At first the sidecars were simply bolted to the frame of the standard solo machine but it wasn't long before the company started to offer machines with special sidecar gearing. This combination is in service with the US Army's 340 Machine Gun Battalion, US Army.(PW)

law-enforcement agencies, a market which was becoming increasingly important to the company.

In mid-1918, the company borrowed $3,000,000 from the Marshall & Ilsley Bank to construct a further extension to the factory. By the time this was completed in April 1920, production was running at 27,040 units per annum. Curiously, the military olive green colour which had been adopted in 1917 was maintained as the standard finish for all machines, regardless of customer, until 1932.

All outstanding military contracts were cancelled in January 1919, at which time the US Army inventory stood at 14,600 Harley-Davidson motorcycles. The army did try out three examples of the horizontally-opposed Model WF 'sport twin' in 1919 but made no further purchases.

By 1920, Harley-Davidson was able to claim that it was the largest manufacturer of motorcycles in the world, and was represented by 2,000 dealers in more than 65 countries.

A year later, the company introduced the 1,213cc (74cu.in) V-twin engine on Models FD and JD but during the same year the factory was temporarily closed due to low sales and managers accepted a 15% cut in pay.

Things appeared to be improving when, in 1922, the company's Export Manager, Alfred Rich Child, signed contracts to supply the Model J to Japan. A year later, Child was nominated as the manager of the first Harley-Davidson dealership in Japan. In July of that year, he negotiated the purchase of 350 so-named 'big twins' to be supplied to the Sankyo Company.

Sales to Japan continued to be important to the company in the decade following the establishment of the dealership. In 1932, a year in which Harley-Davidson built only 7,218 motorcycles and faced an operating loss of $321,670, Child signed a contract worth $32,320 to supply current blueprints, dies and machine tools to the Sankyo Company who would produce Harley-Davidson motorcycles under the name Rikuo. In addition to the one-off payment, an annual royalty

was negotiated for the years 1932 to 1936. For 1935, Sankyo products were said to be of 100% domestic origin. After the fourth and final royalty fee of $10,000 was paid in 1936, Sankyo continued building the motorcycles, supplying a quantity to the Japanese Army under the name Rikuo Type 97. Although motorcycles were rarely taken ashore during the Pacific War, there was, nevertheless, the potential for US soldiers mounted on a Harley-Davidson finding themselves fighting soldiers of the Japanese Imperial Army, some of whom, by a glorious quirk of fate and coincidence were mounted on the Rikou Type 97, a Japanese-built Harley look-alike!

The year 1925 saw the first appearance of the distinctive teardrop-style fuel tank, a design theme continued to this day. Front brakes were first fitted in 1928, having previously been considered dangerous on the less-than perfect road surfaces.

Throughout the 1920s, Harley-Davidson continued to supply motorcycles to the US Army, which then designated

Above: Models F and J were supplied to the US Army in relatively large numbers from 1916. The photograph is of US Army messengers of the Mexican Expeditionary Force mounted on Harley-Davidsons, 15 May 1916.(NA)

Right: A military Model J fitted with leg guards for the rider. Alongside is the ammunition carrier version of the sidecar. (RR/UTX)

'Motorcycle, M1' – the equivalent Indian product being 'Motorcycle , M2' – though both were procured in smaller numbers than had been the case during World War One.

A number of Model FS/LUS combinations appeared in military service in 1922. The first military use of the twin-cam 1,213cc (74cu.in) Model JD solo machine was in 1924. This was followed by the introduction of the Models VL, VD,

VDS and the smaller-engined RL during the years 1930 to 1936. This time the inlet-over-exhaust valve configuration had given way to a side-valve design, albeit the engine capacity remained unchanged at 1,213cc (74cu.in) or 737cc (45cu.in), respectively.

An all-new 737cc (45cu.in) 'Flathead' side-valve engine was first fitted to the 1929 Model D, but Harley-Davidson suffered badly from the 1929 stock market crash and the ensuing depression. It was not until 1933 that the company was beginning to show a modest profit again. Production increased by 150% between 1934 and 1935.

Nevertheless, times remained tough, and attempts were made throughout the 1930s to increase export sales to compensate for the downturn in domestic trade. Motorcycles were supplied to the armies of various South American countries, to Germany, the Netherlands, Spain, China and Scandinavia. Loyalist military cadets, before they were

overrun by Franco's forces, used a Model VL during the Spanish Civil War as a power source for a static generator. A single Model VSC/LC sidecar outfit was supplied to the Swedish Landsverk company in 1932 for conversion to an armoured machine-gun mount for the Danish Army. A modest number of Model VL/LT sidecar combinations were supplied to the Chinese Army in 1933.

In the early 1920s, the Rock Island Arsenal, Illinois constructed a number of experimental cross-country cargo carriers designed to be controlled by a pedestrian walking at the rear and were intended as a support vehicle for use by artillery units. The first prototypes of these machines were two types of aluminium-bodied tracked carts, one with a payload capacity of 300lb (136kg), the other rated at 450lb (204kg), which were produced between 1922 and 1923. Both were powered by a 584cc (36cu.in) Harley-Davidson horizontally opposed two-cylinder engine producing 7.5hp, and driving

the rear sprocket through a three-speed gearbox. Maximum speed was 6mph (10kph). The vehicle could also float when fully loaded. A wheeled version appeared a year or so later, designated the M1924. This machine was fitted with a cargo box at the front and had a rated payload of 450lb (204kg). The engine appears to have been the 1,213cc (74cu.in) unit, with a power output of 18hp; top speed was, of course, limited to that of the driver who was still forced to walk or run behind. The later M1924E version incorporated an articulated steering facility and is thought to have been fitted with the 999cc (61cu.in) engine. No production contract was placed.

The overhead-valve 999cc (61cu.in) Model E – quickly dubbed 'Knucklehead' because of the shape of the rocker covers – was launched in 1936. A year later, in 1937, the soon-to-become legendary Model W, with the smaller 737cc (45cu.in) side-valve engine (once fitted to the Models D and RL) was introduced with the US Army ordering 50 machines.

William Herbert Davidson was named as Vice-President in 1937. Sadly in the same year William A. Davidson, the eldest of the Davidson brothers, died.

By the end of the decade, it was clear that Harley-Davidson had survived what had been very tough times, but the recession had decimated the US motorcycle industry. By 1939, there were just two large manufacturers remaining – Harley-Davidson and their great rival, Indian. However, the uncertain political situation, combined with the prospect of war in Europe was not without opportunity and Indian was the first to benefit, receiving an order for 5,000 combination outfits for the French Army.

With singularly bad timing, Harley-Davidson had launched the Model FL 'Special Sport' in 1941. As soon as the USA entered the war, the production of civilian motorcycles was severely curtailed. Those being produced were in general supplied to police authorities and similar government bodies.

Above: Photographed at Fort Brown, Brownsville, Texas. This photograph shows a splendid line-up of sidecar-equipped machines of the US Motorcycle Corps. Most are equipped with the standard civilian sidecar. To the right of centre is the open platform-type sidecar that Harley-Davidson developed to carry a machine gun. (RR/UTX)

Following pages: The platform-type sidecar designed by William Harley to carry a tripod mounted machine gun. (RR/UTX)

World War Two

In December 1941, soon after the USA's official involvement in World War Two, the Department of Defense placed the first of a series of major contracts with Harley-Davidson which eventually resulted in the supply of 80,000 examples of the solo Model WLA. Derived from the civilian WL of 1937, and powered by the 737cc (45cu.in) engine, WLAs were supplied to all of the Allies under the Lend-Lease arrangements. There was also a special variant produced for Canadian Army,

described as the WLC. Small quantities of the more-powerful Models ELA, FS, UA, UH and US were supplied in solo and combination form, and the US Army also bought four examples of the three-wheeled GA Servi-Car. In addition, 1,600 Model US sidecar twins were delivered to British forces in South Africa in 1942. Although all civilian motorcycle production had ceased on 9 February 1942, the machines supplied to the military were all recognisably derived from pre-war civilian models, with one exception. In 1941, the company produced an experimental military machine known as the Model XA. With its shaft drive and horizontal flat-twin engine of 739cc (45cu.in), the XA was very much in the German mould but, sadly, it never entered series production.

The decline

Although motorcycles were undoubtedly used widely by the US Army throughout World War Two, and in every theatre

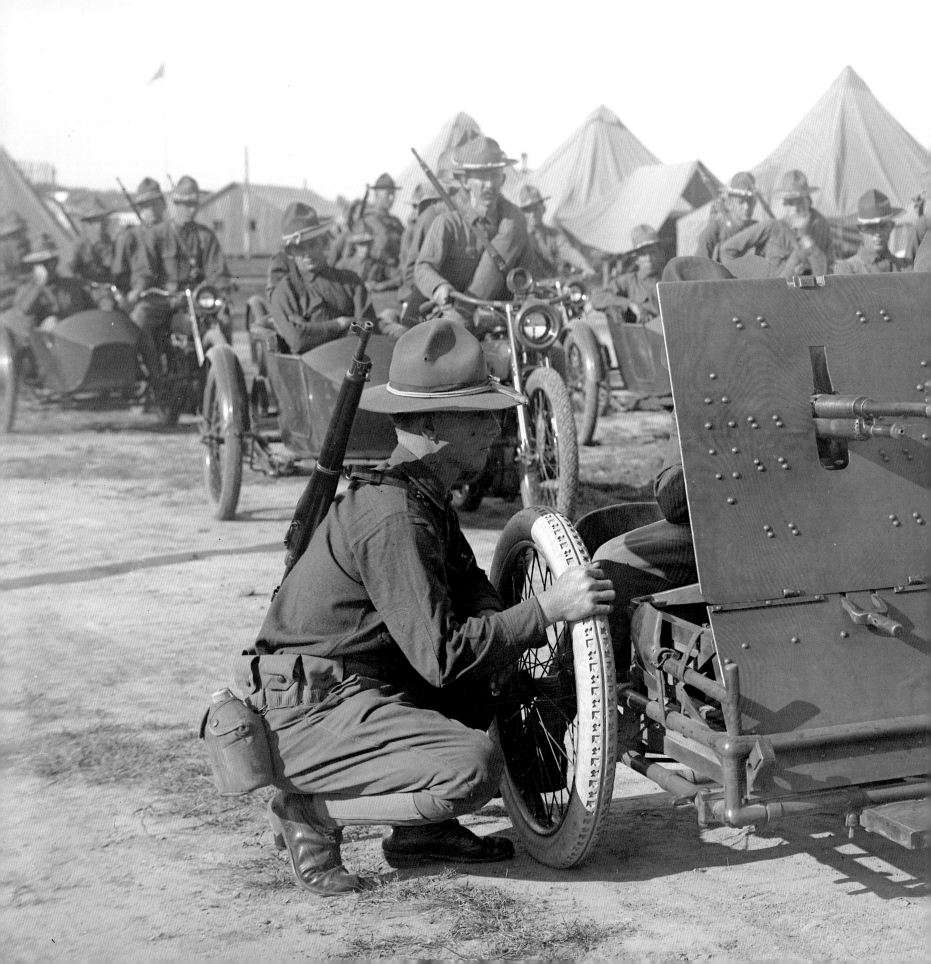

In 1926 single-cylinder machines were
again manufactured by Harley-Davidson
for the first time since 1918. The Models
A, AA and B, BA were produced with
side-valve or overhead-valve engines. This
small machine was named 'Peashooter' by
enthusiasts. (DK)

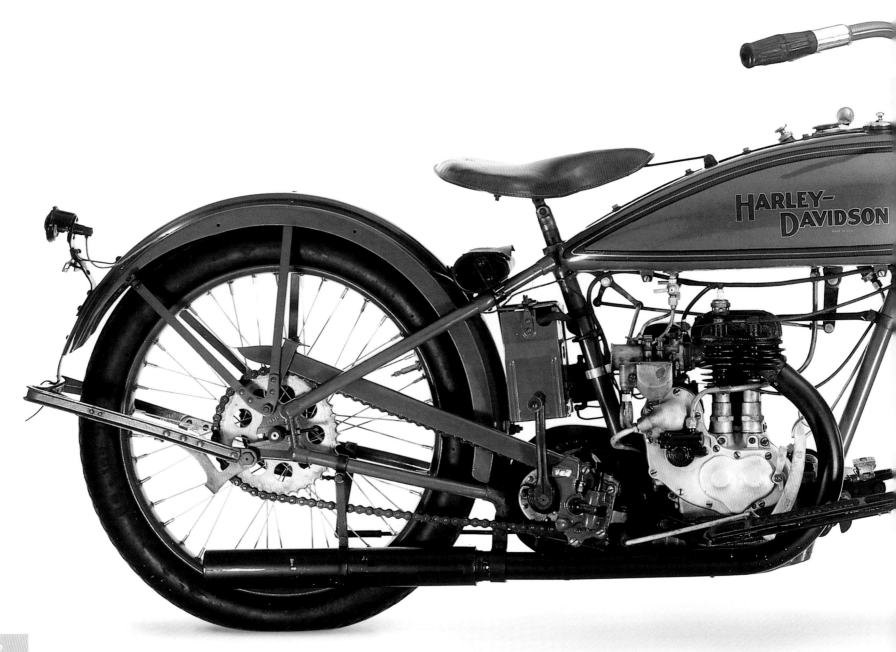

of operation, it must be noted that from approximately mid-1942, they were largely superseded by the ubiquitous Jeep.

For example, standing orders had initially decreed that motorcycles be attached to each armoured division, but this practice came to an end in March 1942 when the type was removed from the Tables of Organization and Equipment (TOE), having been replaced by the Jeep. Of course, this does not mean that motorcycles were not used by armoured units; it simply means they were not authorised. Similarly, motorcycles were not listed in the TOE for field military police (MP) units for the years 1943 to 1945, although camp and station MP units were authorised a maximum of 16 motorcycles (or Jeeps). Airborne divisions continued to use motorcycles, which were authorised at a ratio of two machines per division until the end of December 1944 at which time the figure was increased to 260. These were not necessarily the heavy motorcycles as typified by the products of Harley-Davidson and Indian.

Further indication of the decline in use of the motorcycle is that driver and mechanic courses were terminated in 1943.

Large numbers of motorcycles were disposed of by the US Army in the spring and summer of 1944. When the war in Europe ended in May 1945, thousands of military vehicles were put up for sale in the USA as surplus to requirements. Amongst these were 15,000 WLAs, offered at a government controlled retail price of $450. Many were low-mileage machines which had never left the USA, some were even still crated. A quantity of shaft-drive XAs followed at $500 each. At the same time, large numbers of motorcycles were also offered for sale in Britain through F. H. Warr, Marble Arch Motors and Pride & Clarke. Many being converted to a more luxurious civilian specification.

But, clearly the Army had retained some motorcycles since the number allocated to an MP constabulary regiment was increased to 25 in March 1946. Motorcycles were briefly re-instated to the TOE for armoured divisions in October 1948 at a rate of six motorcycles per division.

Military dead-ends
Aside from the regular production military machines, Harley-Davidson had also been involved with an interesting, and little-known, development project which, had the

development of the Jeep not been so successful, would have resulted in the name Harley-Davidson, rather than Willys, being indelibly associated with military reconnaissance vehicles.

In 1940, at a time when the US Army was testing what was to become the Jeep, Harley-Davidson was contracted to supply 15 examples of a three-seat 'field car' for trials. Designated as Model TA, the vehicle was not dissimilar to the 'Servi-Car' in appearance but with the rear locker replaced by a small bench seat. Smaller-diameter disc wheels were fitted in place of the standard spoked type. The prototype was initially powered by the company's 999cc (61cu.in) 'Knucklehead' engine, driving the rear wheels via a propeller shaft, but it appears that this lacked sufficient power. A single example was modified by increasing engine

Above: Although principally produced for the Canadian Army, the WLC was also used in small numbers by the US Army. (DC/BVMM)

Above right: A WLC with sidecar, the design of which dated back to World War One. (DC/BVMM)

capacity to 1,130cc (69cu.in). Sadly for Harley-Davidson, the Army was impressed by the Jeep, and rapidly lost interest in the field car. There was no further development.

A year later, in 1941, a Model GA 'Servi-Car' was trial-fitted with General Electric radio equipment, as was a UH sidecar combination, although the latter used RCA equipment. No report of the reason for these trials, or the outcome, has so far been uncovered.

There was another interesting military development when, in 1942, the Army Desert Training Center at Indio, California tested a WLA. This had been modified, perhaps by Army personnel, to mount a pair of close-coupled rear wheels which were intended to improve traction. Perhaps unsurprisingly, this experiment was not continued.

In 1943, Willys-Overland, manufacturers of the mighty Jeep, made a contribution to the 'extra lightweight 4x4' project being run by the US Ordnance Corps, with three minimal Jeeps, known as the 'Willys air-cooled' (WAC) or 'Jeeplet'. Power was supplied by a centre-mounted Harley-Davidson clutch and three-speed gearbox engine driving Spicer axles through a differential. The vehicle was capable of 45mph (72.5kph) on the road and could just

tow a 1,000lb (454kg) load. The engine was described as a fan-cooled 180° horizontally-opposed twin with a capacity of 802cc (49cu.in), presumably being a bored-out version of the 739cc (45cu.in) engine of the XA motorcycle. The cooling fan was mounted directly on the front of the crankshaft. The vehicle had independent suspension at the front using transverse springs and permanent four-wheel drive. It was little more than a motorised 'buckboard', with a forward-control driving position and minimal bodywork. Primitive seating for two was fitted in the front and a small cargo box capable of carrying a 500lb (227kg) load at the rear. A third machine was identical except that the front-wheel drive could be disengaged. One of the prototypes ran successfully for 6,627 miles (10,665km) on a scheduled 10,650-mile

Introduced in 1947 the Model FL
'Hydra-Glide' was the first Harley-Davidson
motorcycle to be fitted with hydraulic
(telescopic) front forks. The machine is
fitted with the 'Panhead' engine. (DK)

(17,139km) test course before it failed beyond repair. Other trial vehicles were supplied by Ford, Kaiser, Chevrolet and Crosley but none was considered sufficiently reliable to be put into series production.

Three further lightweight prototypes were constructed by Willys in 1944, under the name WAC-3, using the same engine and drive train, but this time on a platform-type vehicle. Again, there was no series production, but this little vehicle evolved into the postwar M274 Mechanical Mule. Sadly, it was not Harley-Davidson powered.

Between 1944 and 1945, prototype motorcycles were built for the Soviet Army. There was a solo machine based on the WLA and designated 45-WLR. A 3x2 combination outfit was also produced under the designation Model WSR, with a single-seater sidecar carrying a windscreen and spare wheel. Both types were powered by the standard military 737cc (45cu.in) side-valve engine, but neither went into series production. By the end of 1945, the Iron Curtain had fallen.

Post-war years

Civilian production resumed in November 1945, and two years later the company took over the former A. O. Smith propeller plant in Wauwatosa, Wisconsin, for use as a machining facility. Final assembly continued to take place at Juneau Avenue, with components ferried between the two sites. Additional production space was acquired in 1947 at Capitol Drive, Milwaukee.

In 1948, the US Army trialled the Harley-Davidson Model S, a small single-cylinder two-stroke engined machine based heavily on the German-manufactured DKW RT125, the designs for which had been received as part of war reparations.

The Model S was broadly similar to the British-built BSA Bantam, which was also based on the DKW. The Army tested the Model S against the Indian 148, which had been in use as a lightweight airborne machine since 1944. However, this was hardly traditional Harley-Davidson territory, and the Army made no further purchases, continuing to favour the Indian 148, and the later 149M. However, the Model S, which was later upgraded to 165cc, (27cu.in) went on to sell more than 50,000 units in 12 years.

In 1948 both the 999cc (61cu.in) and 1,311cc (80cu.in) engines were fitted with aluminium cylinder heads and hydraulic valve lifters, together with a new-style chrome-plated rocker cover. The shape of the rocker cover gave these engines the 'pan head' nickname. Another improvement, in 1949, was the appearance of hydraulic front forks on the Model E and F 'Hydra-Glides'.

Despite lack of interest in the Model S, and despite having disposed of vast numbers of surplus motorcycles, many of which were almost new, during the immediate post-war years, the US Army continued to buy small numbers of WLAs into the early 1950s. Although none were produced during the three years following the end of the war, 436 machines were supplied in 1949, 15 in 1950, just one in 1951, and possibly two in 1952.

Hendee Manufacturing, owners of the Indian brand, went out of business in 1953. This left Harley-Davidson as the sole US motorcycle manufacturing company, that is until 1999.

The last 'Servi-Cars', now simply described as Model G, and presumably the standard civilian offering, were supplied to the US Army in 1950 for use by Military Police. Motorcycles were officially removed from the US Tables of Organization and Equipment in 1957. The 'Servi-Car' was to remain in production for civilian users until 1973. Motorcycles were not used in either the Korean or Vietnam Wars by US combat troops.

Harley-Davidson's last US military order came in 1963 when some 418 XLH 'Sportsters', designated XLA, were purchased for Military Police and naval shore patrol duties. There were modest sales of military machines to the Netherlands and Belgium in 1956 and 1967, respectively, the latter being the last use of military Harley-Davidsons in Europe.

The US Army started using motorcycles again in the mid-to late 1970s and, although Harley-Davidson submitted some machines for trials, there were to be no further purchases, the army preferring lighter weight lower-cost Japanese motorcycles.

It must have appeared that the general demise of the military motorcycle for all but convoy escort duties,

coupled with the spectacular rise of the Japanese motorcycle industry spelled the end of the military Harley-Davidson. It was to be more than 20 years before the company again became involved in military procurement. When this happened, it was with the British-designed, Rotax-engined MT350 and MT500 motorcycles. In 1987 the company purchased the production rights from Armstrong. Building of these machines, which were supplied to the British, Canadian, Jordanian and US armies, took place at the company's largest assembly plant in York, Pennsylvania.

Meanwhile, the year 1969 had become something of a turning point for the Harley-Davidson brand, when the company changed ownership. Further growth had appeared impossible without a larger partner. Following an attempted hostile take-over by the Bangor Punta Company, and after 68 years in the hands of successive members of the two families, the company was sold to AMF – American Machine & Foundry Company – for $21,000,000. AMF's ownership was not always a happy time and Harley-Davidson motorcycles suffered a magnitude of problems, notably in terms of reliability, with ensuing warranty problems.

In 1973, production was moved to a new 400,000sq. ft (37,160sq.m) plant in York, Pennsylvania, although engines and non-motorcycle products continued to be manufactured in Milwaukee.

In June 1981, a management buy-out saw Harley-Davidson revert to private ownership. Although John Davidson pulled out at the last minute, the board of the new company, now organised into three divisions – Harley-Davidson, Milwaukee, Harley-Davidson, York and Harley-Davidson International – included Vaughn L. Beals Jnr as Chairman and Charles Thompson as President. Willie G. Davidson, the son of the former company's President William H. Davidson and grandson of William A. Davidson was among the 13 executives who purchased the company from AMF.

A near disaster
The new board was faced with the monumental task of updating a tired and unreliable product range in order to turn

Above: The 'Electra-Glide' was a popular mount of many US State Police departments. The machine was also used by a few foreign armies. (DK)

around the fortunes of this once great company. 'Willie G', who had been with the company since 1963, having weathered the AMF years, was appointed Vice-President of styling. However, a year later, Vaughn L. Beals announced that the company was in deep trouble, and facing imminent bankruptcy. Savage retrenchment followed. The company disposed of those aspects of the business that were not considered to be 'core' , such as boats and snowmobiles. Harley-Davidson also laid-off staff, froze salaries and terminated pension and health-care programmes. Even advertising was suspended.

But product development continued and the introduction, in 1985, of the so-called 'Evolution' engine appeared finally to lay the 'ghost' of unreliability to rest. However, 1985 also saw another difficult time when the company's financiers announced that they were going to withdraw support, believing that the venture had become too risky. Harley-Davidson filed for 'Chapter 11' protective administration in January 1986, and worked hard to restructure its considerable debt during that year. A $45 million loan was made by the Heller Finance Group of Chicago. For the first time, later that year, shares were offered to the public. Clearly, the US public saw Harley-Davidson in a somewhat different light to the financiers, and the flotation was so successful that the stock had doubled in value within a year, with the $11 price per share reaching $24 by August 1987.

Above: The Rotax-engined MT500 was originally designed and built by the British Armstrong company but the rights were acquired by Harley-Davidson in 1987. (DK)

Left: The Austrian-built Rotax engine was originally used by Harley-Davidson in their 1970s production trail bikes. (DC/BVMM)

The world wide stock market crash of October that year saw the shares drop below the original $11 issue price and it was to be some time before the price recovered. But the company was well on the way to recovery.

It was to be a long road, but it is testament to the hard work of the board and employees of the new company that Harley-Davidson has not only survived but found new vigour and worldwide sales success. Enthusiasm for the company's products continues to grow and more than 250,000 people attended Milwaukee for the final stop of the 'Open Road Tour' and the company's centenary celebration and party. In 2006, Harley-Davidson unveiled plans for a new museum in Milwaukee, scheduled for opening in 2008.

Refusing to lay down and die, Harley-Davidson has continued to plough its own distinctive furrow, producing handsome, heavy-duty motorcycles which once again have a deserved reputation for rugged reliability.

41

World War One

On 16 March 1916, the US government ordered twelve Model 16-J motorcycles together with a number of sidecars, including a stretcher unit, and special designs for mounting a machine gun and carrying ammunition. The US had yet to enter the war which was raging in France and Belgium and these machines were intended for a different purpose, pursuing Pancho Villa's troops across the border into Mexico. A week or so later, the government ordered a further six Harley-Davidson motorcycles.

CHAPTER 2 WORLD WAR ONE

Many believe that Gottlieb Daimler had invented the first real motorcycle in 1885 and although the machine was really still in its infancy when the first Harley-Davidsons had entered military service in 1916, there had already been significant improvements. By the time the US government started to purchase Harley-Davidsons for the US expeditionary force in Europe, it was clear that the motorcycle was going to replace the horse and rider.

When the USA entered the First World War in 1917, more orders followed and, in an attempt to standardise riding characteristics, the US Army insisted that all motorcycles supplied were to be fitted with right-hand twist-grip throttle and left-hand gearshift, with the lowest gear selected in the forward position. A foot-operated clutch was mounted on the left-hand side and the rear-brake pedal on the right. All nuts, bolts and screws were to be standard sizes to simplify maintenance, as were the chain and tyres. None of this presented a problem for Harley-Davidson whose machines complied in every respect without modification. Harley-Davidson Models F and J were widely used by all of the Allied forces, being fitted with the same 999cc (61cu.in) V-twin engine. The difference between the Model F and J was that the Model F had no battery or electric lighting, relying instead on magneto ignition and acetylene lamps. Whilst the original gray [sic] paint – which the machines had been painted since 1908, giving rise to the name 'The Silent Gray Fellow' – was replaced by a more military olive green finish, the F and J were otherwise standard civilian machines. The military green became the standard finish until the 1928 model year.

Typical roles for which the machines were used included despatch riders, and Military Police in traffic control and escort duties. The machines were also used by communication-line repair teams, supply units, medical personnel, medical evacuation teams and machine-gun crews.

Within a very short time, approximately half of the company's output – which reached a total of 18,522 machines for 1917 and 27,608 for 1918 – was being supplied to the government. Subsequently the company was awarded B-4 status by the government indicating that Harley-Davidson products were essential to the war effort.

Right: The former grey finish having given way to a typical military green, the Harley-Davidson Models J and F were widely used by all of the Allied forces, the J being fitted with electric lighting, the F making do with acetylene gas. Major-General George W. Read carries out an inspection at the Motor Overhaul Park, Le Mans, France, 5 April 1919. (NA)

Previous page: With its big twin-cylinder engine, three-speed transmission and electric lighting, the chain-drive Model J was widely used by the Allied forces. Here, a frozen rider waits whilst a camera is unloaded from a British Sopwith 1¹/₂ Strutter reconnaissance aircraft. (NA)

Training of both military riders and mechanics proved to be something of a problem, subsequently training schools were set up under the auspices of the US government. The Harley-Davidson training facility was established by Joseph Ryan and started operation in July 1917, eventually processing some 300 military personnel in the following 16 months. The operation continued after 1918 as a dealer training school.

After 1917, there was no further export to the Japanese Army, although this was by no means the last dealings which the company was to have with Japan.

A report entitled 'America's Munitions', published in 1919 by the Assistant Secretary of War, stated that 'The need of the Army for motorcycles, sidecars and bicycles was so tremendous that for many months during the war practically the entire output of these vehicles most suitable for Army use was taken by the Government. It was found that the Indian and Harley-Davidson motorcycles were best adapted to meet the necessities of the US Expeditionary Forces in France and these types were standardized for overseas shipment.'

Most Harley-Davidson company histories tell how the first US soldier into Germany at the end of World War One was Corporal Roy Holtz of Chippewa Falls, Wisconsin, who happened to be riding a Harley-Davidson motorcycle

Above: Flanked by an early White armoured car (designated 'armoured car number 2' by the US Army), this fine line-up of Model F and J motorcycles shows the standard passenger sidecar of the period together with examples of the machine-gun mounting and ammunition sidecars.(RR/UTX)

Right: Harley-Davidson mounted US Cavalrymen, known as the 'Speed Boys', at Camp Sherman, Chillicothe, Ohio in 1918. (PW)

combination. On the 8/9 November 1918, it appears that Holtz was detailed to take his captain on a reconnaissance mission in northern Belgium; the pair managed to get lost and ended up asking for directions at a farmhouse, which they discovered was being used as a German Army billet and they were promptly taken prisoner. Both were released when

the Armistice was declared on 11 November but the historic ride was re-enacted for the camera a day later, albeit Holtz was rumoured to be riding in the wrong direction!

The report on American Munitions referred to above also stated that by 1 November 1918, a total of 12,376 Harley-Davidson motorcycles had been delivered, along with 14,054 manufactured by Indian. In total, 20,007 motorcycles of the two manufacturers had been shipped overseas by the end of the war. Other sources suggest that by the end of 1918, Harley-Davidson had supplied 18,018 motorcycles to the US Army, as well as 16,804 sidecars. Nevertheless, for all but the last six months of the war US civilian customers could continue to buy Harley-Davidson motorcycles.

Along with the other motorcycle manufacturers in the USA, Harley-Davidson was requested by the War Department to contribute to the design of a standard military motorcycle. The company's contribution was a V-twin 999cc (61cu.in) engined model, but the project never reached any conclusion.

Model J

The Model J was the first Harley-Davidson to be supplied to the US Army in quantity. First delivered in 1915 and initially designated 11-J, the machine carried a price tag of $310. It was among the company's most successful early models, selling a very creditable 3,719 units in the first year of production and more than 85,000 during a 15-year life. Power was provided by the 999cc (61cu.in) V-twin four-stroke engine which had been introduced on the Model X-8-E in 1912; inlet valves were in the cylinder head, whilst the exhaust valves were in the cylinder casting. Drive to the rear wheel was via an adjustable multi-plate clutch, new-type three-speed transmission and open chain. The new transmission meant

The first Yank and Harley Davidson to enter Germany. 11/12/18

Above: The first US soldier into Germany during the Great War was Corporal Roy Holtz of Chippewa Falls, Wisconsin, who was captured with his captain during a reconnaissance trip in Belgium on 8/9 November 1918. Both were released when the armistice was declared on 11 November but the historic ride on Holtz's Harley was re-enacted for the camera a day later. (PW)

that the machine offered considerably better performance than earlier models.

Announcement of the Model J was made in the autumn of 1914 and was billed as the top of the range model. The new transmission made better use of the engine's power output characteristics and the fact that the gearbox was now mounted immediately behind the engine, rather than in the rear hub, gave a better overall weight distribution, improving handling. Engine power output was also improved – increased by some 37% when compared to the previous year. The cycle-type pedals which had previously been used as a means of starting, were finally removed and replaced by an inertia-type kickstarter.

Superficially, the Model J was similar in many respects to earlier models but the company announced that it included 98 separate improvements in design. These included lubrication by 'automatic' oil pump, albeit the used oil was then either burned or dripped on the ground using the usual total-loss system of the period. The new transmission was of the sliding-gear type, with all of the mechanism enclosed in oil, and for the first time, the primary and secondary drive chains were now placed on the same side of the engine. An interlock was fitted which prevented the rider from operating the gear change without first having disengaged the clutch. A gate for the gear-change lever was mounted on the side of the petrol tank.

For the 1916 model, the naming convention was changed to include the actual year of production as a prefix to the model identification rather than using a consecutive number. Instead of being described as 12-J, the model description became 16-J and then 17-J, 18-J onwards. Engineering changes for the year included a rounding of the fuel tank

Above: A makeshift motorcycle workshop of the 2nd Field Battalion Signals Corps at Bonvillers, France, 20 May 1918. Whilst the machine nearest to the camera is a Harley-Davidson others are clearly of Indian manufacture. (NA)

Left: Despatch riders of the 88th Division Headquarters troop ready for duty at Lagney, Meurthe et Moselle, France, 22 November 1918. The first machine is an Indian and the second a Harley-Davidson. (NA)

Previous pages: Harley-Davidson's great rival during the early part of the 20th century was the Hendee-Indian company of Springfield, Massachusetts. The machine to the left, parked in front of the Model T Ford, is an Indian Powerplus. On the move, is a Harley-Davidson Model J of the US Army Traffic Police in Paris, 21 April 1919. (NA)

edges, wider front forks and a front mudguard. Stronger wheel rims, improved front hub bearings and a larger headstock bearing was fitted. Engine valve seats were now cut to a new 45° angle. The same frame and footboards were adopted for all of the company's models.

The price was reduced to $295, and sales for the year amounted to 5,898 units.

Standard (civilian) sidecars, which were built by the Seaman Company, had initially included the Model 11-L, a single-passenger right-hand sidecar, the L-11-L, which was intended for left-hand attachment, and the 11-M commercial box sidecar. Other types were added as production continued.

Special military-pattern sidecars were introduced for 1916, including the 16-GC, designed by William S. Harley with a machine-gun mounting behind a folding armoured screen and a small seat for the gunner. The sidecar could mount the Colt-Browning Model 1904, the Model 1917 machine gun or the Browning 'automatic rifle' of 1918. Also the British-made drum-fed Lewis machine gun. Other military sidecars included the 16-AC ammunition car, also the 16-SC ambulance, on which the casualty was carried at saddle height on a built-in stretcher.

The year 1916 was when the US Army first purchased Harley-Davidson motorcycles.

From 1916, the US Army ordered large quantities of the Model J for shipment overseas. Also from this year, regardless of the end user, the red-striped Renault-style grey finish

Above: Although Harley-Davidson was later to become the sole US manufacturer of motorcycles during World War One, more were actually produced by Hendee-Indian. By 1 November 1918, 12,376 Harley-Davidson motorcycles had been delivered, along with 14,054 Indians. The photograph shows an Indian Powerplus 'heavy motorcycle with sidecar' of the 6th US Marines, 2nd Divison leaving headquarters at Sommedieue, France, 30 April 1918. (NA)

Right: The days of reliable and portable radio communications were far distant when this Harley-Davidson rider was photographed with a carrier pigeon basket. The machine is almost certainly a Model F. The rider is about to deliver the messenger birds to advanced positions in Mesnil-St Fermin, France, 2 May 1918. (NA)

Above: Pigeons continued to provide a valuable means of sending messages well into the 1930s. This is a Model J, photographed at Fort Shafter, Hawaii, June 1930. (NA)

Right: The headquarters of the 17th Brigade, US Army at Grande Rue, Lucey, Meurthe et Moselle, France, 20 November 1919. (NA)

which had been used for the tank, frame and mudguards, was replaced by olive green. The engine crankcase was similarly painted olive green. Other changes to the machine were minimal, but the engine timing was altered to increase valve overlap. Both the inlet housing and exhaust manifold were improved; also the Remy magneto was replaced by a Dixie unit. The price was raised to $310 and sales totalled 9,180 units; with around half of all Model J production in 1917 going to the US military.

Changes for 1918 were minimal but, for the first time, all Model J machines were fitted with a Remy magneto generator system. This provided the ignition spark and powered an electrical headlight, tail light and horn. A vacuum-operated battery cut-out disconnected the system when the throttle

was closed. Some 6,500 Model Js were built during the year, with the price now increased to $320.

Small changes were made to the clutch-operating mechanism for 1919. Handlebar and width was increased by 2½in (64mm). For the first time, a dedicated sidecar version of the Model J, known as the JS featuring a lower compression

Left: The squared edges to the fuel tank and the cycle-type pedals suggest that this is a 1915 Model F or J. This was the first year of the new three-speed transmission. The rider is a Sergeant Pilot of the Royal Flying Corps. (RAFM)

Right and below: Introduced in 1915 and remaining in the catalogue until 1929, the Model J (and the similar Model F) was widely used by the US Army as well as by other allies during the First World War. A total of 85,500 were built. (DK)

Technical specification

Models J, JS.

Engine:
999cc (61cu.in) Harley-Davidson '61'; two cylinders @ 45° 'V' formation; bore and stroke, 3.3in x 3.5in (84 x 89mm); overhead inlet, side exhaust valves; total-loss lubrication; air cooled; power output, 11bhp at 3,000rpm.

Transmission:
3F; hand gear-change; multi-plate dry clutch; exposed roller-chain drive to rear wheel; primary and secondary chains on left-hand side of the engine.

Suspension:
parallelogram leading-link steel-tube front forks with a single coil spring; solid rear forks.

Brakes:
Mechanically operated expanding band; rear only until 1928, and then front and rear using expanding shoes at front.

Tyre size:
3.00-28 (1914 to 1925), 3.30-26 (1926 to 1927), 3.85-25 (1928 to 1929), same size front and rear.

Construction:
cycle type steel-tube frame.

Electrical system:
6V battery.

Dimensions
(1916 model)
Length, 7ft 8in (2.34m); *width*, 30in (76cm); *height*, 30in (76cm).

Wheelbase, 59.5in (1.5m).
Ground clearance, 4.5in (114mm).
Unladen weight, 325 lb (147.4kg).

Performance
Maximum allowable speed, 60mph (96.6kph).

Range of action
n/a.

Average fuel consumption
n/a.

Comprehensive performance and dimensional data was not always available for militarised civilian models.

ratio and revised gearing better suited to sidecar work was introduced. Both the J and the JS were priced at $370, a considerable increase, but nevertheless, production increased to 9,941 units.

The number of Model Js produced increased again in 1920, to 14,192, the most important change for the year being the use of Harley-Davidson manufactured generators and ignition coils. The introduction of the larger-capacity Model JD in 1921 (see page 66) saw net sales of the Model J fall to 4,526 units, although the price increased to $485. Modifications for the year included the adoption of a solid flywheel, revised pistons and connecting rods. A revised petrol tank, new front and rear mudguards also a front stand were fitted.

In 1922 new inlet and exhaust valves, revised front forks and a manual generator cut-out were incorporated. Production fell again in favour of the larger-engine machines to 3,183 units but the price was also down, at $365. A year later, silicon-chrome metal exhaust valves were fitted. Other improvements included a hinged rear mudguard to make

wheel removal easier and a larger capacity generator. The price was reduced again, to $305, and production for the year stood at 4,802 units.

For 1924, aluminium pistons were introduced and the Models J and JS were redesignated as the JE and JES. Also a new four-plate battery, a better-balanced flywheel and a larger capacity generator were fitted. Both models, still bearing the designations JE and JES, were significantly redesigned the following year (1925) with a lower, wider frame incorporating a steel channel as an engine mount. A distinctive teardrop-shaped fuel tank and new mudguards were fitted. Iron-alloy pistons and a wealth of engineering improvements almost made the JE a brand-new machine. Considering this was, by now, a 10-year old design, this was quite an achievement. As well as providing improved performance and reliability, the appearance of the motorcycle was enhanced considerably. The price remained steady at $315, but sadly it was not enough to arrest the downward slide of sales, with the year's total ending at 4,114 machines sold.

Left: Motorcycles offered better off-road performance than the motor cars of the period and were widely used, for example, for despatch-rider duties. War surplus machines are being inspected by Brigadier-General Walker prior to disposal at Le Mans, France, 5 April 1918. (NA)

Above right: US Motorcycle Corps at Fort Brown, Texas, May 1918. Note the early type of US Army armoured car manufactured by the White Motor Company. (RR/UTX)

Previous pages: Damaged and war surplus machines awaiting disposal or repair at the US Army Engineer Corps overhaul park at Le Mans, France, 5 April 1919. (NA)

The designations reverted to Model J and JS in 1926, and changes included the use of larger-section balloon tyres on a smaller wheel rim, a new silencer and new mudguards (again!). Improvements to the electrical system included a higher-capacity battery, higher-output generator and automatic relay cut-out in place of the vacuum type. The price was unchanged but this was not sufficient to reverse the downward slide in sales which stood at 3,749 units for the year. The headlamp wiring was simplified in 1927. A new distributor-less ignition system was adopted which used a circuit-breaker and a single coil to produce a spark at each cylinder on every up-stroke. The price was reduced to $310, but sales further declined to 3,561.

By 1928, the Model J was ageing and, in a last-ditch attempt to update the model, a front-wheel brake was added and the wheel diameter was reduced again. A number of engineering changes were incorporated, designed to improve reliability, including the use of strengthening gussets at the frame connections. For the first time, the machine acquired an electrical switch panel which included an ammeter. A new high-frequency horn and an adjustable output controller for the generator were fitted. The engine now had an air cleaner. Sales improved briefly, to a figure of 4,184 for 1928, but were down to 2,886 during the last year (1929) of production. The price remained at $310.

Production of the Models J and JS ended in 1929, after a total of 85,500 machines had been manufactured. Whilst never a pure military motorcycle, the Model J was widely used by the US Army during and after World War One, as well as also seeing service with the Dutch, Russian and possibly British armies.

Related models

Similar models which may also have seen limited military service were the Model F, which had been in production since 1913, initially with two-speed transmission, known as the 9-F, and then from 1915 with the three-speed transmission. The Model FS was fitted with sidecar gearing and was offered from 1919. In all respects, these Models F and FS were identical to the Model J but had magneto ignition and no electric lighting equipment.

Production of the Models F and FS ended in 1925.

A specially produced 'government only' version of the Model F was produced in 1918 and 1919. Known as the Model FUS, it was effectively a Model F, equipped with Presto-Lite electric equipment. The total number produced was 15,616. The Model E was similar to the Model F, but retained single-speed transmission and was only in production until 1918.

Inter-war Years

With the development of powerful engines, and the universal inclusion of features such as reliable front suspension, electric lighting and front-wheel brakes, the motorcycle came of age during the inter-war years. Despite a superficial resemblance, in truth there was little commonality between the motorcycles which Uncle Sam's 'doughboys' had ridden at the end of World War One, and those with which they rode to war against Hitler's Germany.

3

Harley-Davidson's product offer for 1919 was little different to that which had been available during World War One, consisting largely of the Models F and J and the horizontally-opposed Model W. In late 1920 the company was in a position to produce something new and even then it was confined to a new 1,213cc (74cu.in) V-twin engine to supplement the original 999cc (61cu.in) unit which had been introduced in 1915. These were identified as the Models FD and JD.

Introduced in 1921, the Model JD, known as the 'Superpower Twin', and the sidecar equivalent, JDS, was intended to compete on equal terms with the big motorcycles being produced by Indian and Henderson. Although, in truth, the JD was effectively little more than the standard Model J, which had been fitted with a larger, 1,213cc (74cu.in) V-twin engine, to provide an increase in performance. The engine was similar in design to the 999cc (61cu.in) unit fitted to the Model J, retaining the same inlet-over-exhaust valve configuration, but both the bore and stroke were increased to provide the 1,213cc (74cu.in) capacity. Many of the major components were completely new, including the cylinders, cylinder heads and crankcase. The transmission would also have been recognised by anyone familiar with the three-speed gearbox used on the Model J. This was housed in a separate aluminium casing and connected to the crankshaft via a primary chain. Final drive to the rear wheel was by the standard exposed chain.

Like the Model J, the JD was equipped with a complete electrical system, comprising a 6V battery, generator and contact-breaker coil ignition system. A horn was fitted along with head and tail lights.

The frame was essentially the standard type already in use on the Model J, comprising a single loop to support the engine. The front forks incorporated suspension by means of twin parallelogram leading-links, with a single coil spring. The rear forks were un-sprung, but the rider was insulated from the worst of the primitive road surfaces by a fully-sprung Mesinger leather saddle. Brakes were provided at the rear only until 1928 when, for the first time, a front brake was fitted, controlled by a handlebar-mounted lever on the left.

The Model JDS, offered at the same time as the solo JD, was intended for sidecar use and this was reflected in the

Previous pages: The appearance of early Jeeps tell us that this photograph was taken in 1941, but the combination of M3 wheeled armoured cars, reconnaissance vehicles and motorcycles is typical of US Army thinking in the late 1930s and into early years of World War Two. The iconic Model WLA motorcycle was essentially pre-war in design, being derived from the 1937 Model WL and the Model DLD of 1930. (NA)

Right: Although it dated back to 1915, the Model F and J continued in production, largely unchanged, until 1928. This is a magneto-equipped Model FS with acetylene lighting; the distinctive sidecar is intended for carrying ammunition. For some reason, the rider is a US Army Military Policeman. (PW)

Above: This is a magneto-equipped Model F, fitted with a leather rifle scabbard, military-type front mudguard and finished in all-over olive drab. Note the more-rounded cylinder-head cooling fins introduced in 1920. (An)

Left: Model FS equipped with an artillery-wheeled machine-gun sidecar; the gun is a water-cooled Browning M1917 belt-fed heavy machine gun. (PW)

gearing. From the second year of production a steel spacer was fitted between the cylinder casting and the head to reduce the compression ratio.

Sales in the first year of production amounted to 2,321 units, and the figure was up to 3,988 the following year when the price was reduced to $390.

Silicon-chrome metal exhaust valves were adopted for 1923, along with improved cylinder heads (now with squarer cooling fins) and a larger-capacity generator. As with the Model J, the rear mudguard was hinged to make wheel removal easier. By now, the machines were priced at $330 and sales for the year stood at 7,458 units which was a very creditable near-100% increase on sales over the previous year.

Although the use of cast-iron pistons continued during 1924, buyers were also offered the option of the aluminium-alloy type. This attracted a $10 surcharge on the $335 price and changed the designations to JDCA and JDSCA. Other changes for the year included a better-balanced flywheel, larger generator, revised front mudguard and a four-plate battery. The production total for the year was 9,003.

Piston material was changed again in 1925 to iron alloy, which resulted in the model designations becoming JDCB and JDCBS. This was also the year in which the distinctive teardrop-style fuel tank was introduced. At the same time, the frame was strengthened by the use of double-butting on the steering tube and the engine mount was modified making

use of a steel channel section. Frame height was reduced by lowering the saddle by 3in (76mm), giving the machine a much more modern appearance. The wheels were reduced in diameter whilst the tyre section was increased.

The appearance was enhanced further in 1926 when the wheel rim diameter was again reduced. The year 1926 also

Above: The company offered a range of sidecars including passenger and commercial designs; this is a typical package sidecar designed for rural deliveries. The motorcycle is a Model JD. (PW)

Right: Harley-Davidson was always keen to demonstrate the speed and reliability of its products in racing. Some owners were equally keen to see what their machines were capable of. These intrepid riders, with their caps reversed, are mounted on a Model JD and look to be set for a bit of off-roading. (DA)

Left: Detroit Police Department had been the first such agency to purchase a Harley-Davidson back in 1908 and sales to law enforcement agencies became increasingly important to the company over the years. This well-turned out officer is sitting astride a 1,213cc (74cu.in) side-valve Model V, which had been introduced in 1929 for the 1930 model year. (DA)

saw improvements to the exhaust system to deflect gases away from the rider and further changes were made to the mudguards. Improvements to the electrical system included a higher-capacity battery, higher-output generator and automatic relay cut-out in place of the vacuum type. The price was unchanged at $335, but sales were up again at 9,544 units.

For 1927, the JD was fitted with the so-called 'wasted spark' ignition system which negated the need for a distributor by using a circuit-breaker and a single coil; this meant that both spark plugs fired together. The headlight wiring was also simplified. The price was reduced to $320 and sales rose again, to 9,691 units.

In parallel with the similar changes made to the smaller-engined Model J in 1928, the JD acquired an engine air cleaner and a front-wheel brake. A number of engineering changes were designed to improve reliability, including the use of reinforcing gussets at joints in the frame. A total of 11,007 examples were built during the year and the price remained at $320. Production for both the JD and the JDS models ended in 1929. Small changes were made during the year and, for the first time, the machine acquired an electrics switch panel which included an ammeter, a new high-frequency horn and an adjustable output controller for the generator. Production dropped back when compared to the previous year, with 10,182 machines built. The price was held at $320.

The US Marines had taken delivery of a small number of virtually-stock civilian Model JD solo machines in 1926 for Military Police and escort duties. White-wall tyres were apparently the order of the day on motorcycles required for ceremonial duties.

Total production for the Models JD and JDS during the nine-year run finished at 66,652.

Related models

The FD and FDS were similar models which may also have seen limited military service. Produced between 1921 and 1925, these were identical to the Models JD and JDS, respectively, but had magneto ignition and no electric lighting equipment.

Model V

Launched in 1930, Harley-Davidson's Model V was powered by a supposedly improved version of the 1,213cc (74cu.in) V-twin side-valve engine, with cylinder heads designed by Harry Ricardo. It was intended to replace the Model JD, but, uncharacteristically, was an initial disaster. Despite the new engine offering 15% more power than the similarly-dimensioned unit which had been fitted to the JD, the Model V weighed something like 100lbs (45.4kg) more, and suffered a myriad of problems into the bargain. The flywheel was too small which allowed lively acceleration at low speeds, but also led to unacceptable vibration. Worse still, exhaust silencers quickly became clogged which choked the engine, the new, lower frame was weak and the clutch poor. The problems were so bad that the first 1,326 examples of the new Model V had to be dismantled and reassembled with improved engines. On the plus side, from 1930 all Harley-Davidsons used quickly-detachable wheels which allowed easier replacement or repair in the event of a puncture. Although the problems were quickly sorted out, and the Model V became as reliable as any that had gone before, the problems did not help Harley-Davidson's financial position as the company attempted to ride out the depression.

The Model V range quickly grew to become the most complex that had been offered so far, and included sufficient models and options to create considerable confusion. The 1930 offering was simple enough, comprising the Model V motorcycle; the Model VL, fitted with higher compression heads; the VS with medium-compression heads and sidecar gearing; and the VC, a so-called 'commercial' model with low-compression heads and nickel-iron rather than aluminium-alloy pistons. The inclusion of an 'M' code in the model designation indicated the use of a magneto rather than a generator system (eg, Model VCM). The launch price was $340, with a total of 10,025 sold in the first year, during which a huge number of improvements were designed and incorporated to counter unreliability.

The standard single-passenger sidecar throughout the run was the Model LT, except for the last year of production when this was changed to the Model K.

Technical specification

Models JD, JDS.

Engine:

1,213cc (74cu.in) Harley-Davidson '74'; two cylinders in 45° 'V' formation; bore and stroke, 3.4in x 4.0in (87mm x 102mm); overhead inlet, side exhaust valves; total-loss lubrication; air cooled; power output, 24bhp at 4,500rpm.

Transmission:

3F; hand gear-change; multi-plate dry clutch; exposed roller-chain drive to rear wheel; primary and secondary chains on left-hand side of the engine.

Suspension:

parallelogram leading-link steel-tube front forks with single coil spring; solid rear forks.

Brakes:

mechanically operated drum brakes; rear only until 1928, then front and rear.

Tyre size:

3.00-28 (1921 to 1924), 3.85-27 (1925 only), 3.30-26 (1926 to 1927) 3.85-25 (1928 to 1929), same size front and rear.

Construction:

cycle type steel-tube frame.

Electrical system:

6V battery.

Dimensions

Length, 97in (2.5m); *width*, 36.5in (93cm); *height*, n/a.

Wheelbase, 59.5in (1.5m).
Ground clearance, n/a.
Unladen weight, 405lb (184kg).

Performance

Maximum allowable speed, 75mph (121kph).
Range of action, n/a.
Average fuel consumption, n/a.

Comprehensive performance and dimensional data was not always available for militarised civilian models.

Technical specification

Models V, VC, VL, VS, etc.

Engine:
1,213cc (74cu.in) Harley-Davidson '74'; two cylinders in 45° 'V' formation; bore and stroke, 3.4in x 4.0in (87mm x 102mm); overhead inlet side exhaust valves; total-loss lubrication; air cooled; power output, 30bhp at 4,000rpm. Models VDDS, VLDD, VLH, VHS, VFH, VHHS (1935/36) fitted with 1,311cc (80cu.in) engine; bore and stroke, 3.4in x 4.25in (87mm x 108mm).

Transmission:
3F; hand gear-change; multi-plate dry clutch; duplex primary chain running in closed casing; exposed roller-chain drive to rear wheel; primary and secondary chains on left-hand side of the engine.

Suspension:
parallelogram leading-link steel-tube front forks with single coil spring; solid rear end.

Brakes:
mechanically operated drum brakes; expanding shoe at front, contracting band at rear.

Tyre size:
3.50-19 (4.00-19 and 4.50-19 available as an option), same size front and rear.

Construction:
cycle type steel-tube frame.

Electrical system:
6V battery.

Dimensions
Length, 88in (2.24m); *width*, 76in (1.9 m); *height*, n/a. *Wheelbase*, 60in (1.53m). *Ground clearance*, 4.1in (104mm). *Unladen weight*, 529lb (240kg).

Performance
Maximum allowable speed, 90mph (145kph). Range of action, n/a. Average fuel consumption, n/a.

Comprehensive performance and dimensional data was not always available for militarised civilian models.

Left: The Model V was the first of Harley-Davidson's products to use a side-valve engine in place of the old F head twin; other changes made at the time included the adoption of a duplex primary chain and forged I-beam front forks. Producing around 22bhp from its 1,213cc (74cu.in), the engine was both strong and reliable. (DC/BVMM))

Right: In 1932, a Model VSC/LC sidecar outfit was supplied to the Swedish Landsverk company for conversion to an armoured machine gun mount for the Danish Army. It was probably not a very competent performer. (PW)

For 1931, the range was expanded to include a special model designed for road marking (Model VCR) and the VMG which used a magneto generator. A new transmission, offering three speeds plus reverse, was offered as an option from mid-year across the range, and there were various engineering improvements. The price remained at $340, regardless of the model selected, but the reputation for unreliability, combined with the effects of the world-wide recession, kept total sales down to 6,790.

There was some rationalisation in 1932 when the 'M' option variants were deleted from the catalogue but, of course, there were the inevitable detail changes, including heavier-duty front forks. The price was reduced to $320, but production slumped to 4,635.

A so-called 'Special Sport' model was introduced in 1933, using magnesium-alloy pistons and high-compression heads; this was described as the Model VLD; there was also a similarly-equipped Model VLE. Other model variations included the VE and the sidecar equivalent VSE. The engine on both models was fitted with magnesium-alloy pistons but presumably with the medium-compression heads. The engine on the VF and the sidecar VFS was fitted with nickel-iron pistons. A further reduction in price to $310 (except the Model VLD which was $320) was not sufficient to boost sales, which stood at just 2,172.

For 1934, all models received an improved lubrication system and the frames and front forks were reinforced. Magnesium-alloy pistons were replaced by aluminium-alloy which improved reliability. The 1934 model line-up included the high-compression VLD, the low-compression VD and sidecar VDS. The engine in the VFD and the sidecar

equivalent VFDS, were both fitted with nickel-iron pistons. Still priced at $310, total sales for the 'year' – which ran for 16 months including four months of 1933 – amounted to 7,555 the majority of which were of the Model VLD.

The 1935 catalogue offered customers a choice of the Models VLD, VD, VDS, VFD, VFDS; there was also a new competition model known as the VLDJ. Late in the year, the range was expanded further to include the VLDD and VDDS, these consisting essentially of a VLD or VDS fitted with a new 1,311cc (80cu.in) engine. The price of 'standard' machines was $320, with the larger-engined models carrying a premium; production across the range was down to 6,385, the majority, again, being the VLD.

There was little change for 1936, the last year of manufacture, but the Model VLDD was replaced by the VLH, whilst the VDDS was replaced by the VHS, again both were equipped with the 1,311cc (80cu.in) engine. The VFH and the sidecar equivalent VFHS, were also equipped with the larger engine with nickel-iron pistons fitted. The range was also expanded to include the VMG, which was fitted with a Bosch magneto. Prices were unchanged at $320 and $340, according to the engine fitted. Total production for the year was 5,480.

Out of this bewildering complexity, the Models VL, VS and VDS certainly saw military use, in the USA and China, the latter using a number of Model VL with the single-passenger Model LT sidecar fitted on the left-hand side. A number of examples of the Model VS were supplied to Denmark in 1934 for trials against Danish-manufactured Nimbus, also fitted with LT sidecars. At least one of the Harley-Davidson was fitted with an armoured sidecar by Landsverk in Sweden, designed to mount a machine gun; this was designated Landsverk 210 but did not enter into series production.

Total production of the Model V during the seven-year production run was 43,042.

Model G 'Servi-Car'

First made available in 1932, the three-wheeled Model G 'Servi-Car' has the distinction of being Harley-Davidson's longest-running model, with some 32,000 constructed during the 42-year production run. The machine was originally aimed at service stations who, Harley-Davidson believed, would use it to pick-up or deliver motorcars for servicing or repair. It was sold on the basis that a lone mechanic could drive the 'Servi-Car' to the location in question and then simply attach it to the back bumper of the motorcar being picked-up by means of the special tow bar, thus returning to base without the need for a second driver. It was clearly an acceptable idea because Harley-Davidson's great rivals, the Indian Motorcycle Company, launched their own version, the 'Dispatch-Tow', a year later.

Above: Introduced in 1932, the Model GA 'Servi-Car' has the distinction of being Harley-Davidson's longest-running model. It was originally aimed at service stations who, Harley-Davidson believed, would use it to pick-up or deliver motor cars for servicing or repair, the trike being attached by a special towbar to the rear of the car. A small number were used in military service but not in the role which the company had envisaged. (DA)

At first glance the model does not exactly accord with the modern Harley image, but the 'Servi-Car' was effectively the front end of a heavy motorcycle, with the frame extended and adapted at the rear to mount a standard car-type rear axle, with a fully-enclosed differential. A small locker compartment over the rear axle provided space for storing

From the outset, the 'Servi-Car' was offered in four different variants. The basic vehicle was the Model G, supplied with the special tow bar, which could be stowed on the rear compartment when not required. The Model GA was identical but did not include the tow bar – in Harley-Davidson designations, an 'A' suffix generally denoted 'army' but not in this case. The GD had a larger-capacity rear compartment

tools or other equipment. Mudguards were attached to the sides of the compartment to cover the rear wheels. Early examples could be purchased with a padded bench seat over the storage box. The 'Servi-Car' was a surprisingly handsome, stylish and useful vehicle with more than a hint of art-deco styling, and had the advantage of being easily operated by personnel who were not familiar with riding a motorcycle.

The 'Servi-Car' was also available without the special tow bar and, in this condition, became much favoured by small storekeepers for deliveries. The machine was also used by parking enforcement officers and police in metropolitan areas. A small number of 'Servi-Cars' was also purchased by the US Army, both during and after World War Two.

Technical specification

Models G, GA 'Servi-Car'.

Engine:
737cc (45cu.in) Harley-Davidson '45'; two cylinders in 45° 'V' formation; bore and stroke, (1932 to 1935) 2.9in x 3.2in (73mm x 81mm), (1936 to 1973) 2.8in x 3.9in (70mm x 98mm); side valves; dry sump; air cooled; power output, 22–23bhp at 4,600rpm; torque, 28lbf/ft at 3,000rpm.

Transmission:
3F1R (no reverse included for 1932 to 1933 models); hand gear-change; multi-plate dry clutch; duplex primary roller-chain running in closed casing; exposed roller-chain drive to rear axle.

Suspension:
parallelogram leading-link steel-tube front forks with single coil spring; rear axle suspended on twin quarter-elliptical cantilevered multi-leaf springs, with rubber bump stops; rear body suspended on helical coil springs.

Brakes:
drum brakes; front and rear; mechanically operated (to 1950); hydraulic drum brakes (1950 to 1972); hydraulic disc brakes (1973 only).

Tyre size:
5.00-16, same size front and rear.

Construction:
steel-tube frame.

Electrical system:
6V battery.

Dimensions
Length, 107in (2.72m); *width*, 52in (1.3m); *height*, 52in (1.3m). *Wheelbase*, 61in (1.6m). *Rear track*, 42in (1.10m). *Ground clearance*, 4.5in (114mm). *Unladen weight*, 1,360lb (617kg).

Performance
Maximum allowable speed, 45mph to 65mph (72kph to 105kph). Range of action, 120 miles (193km). Average fuel consumption, 40mpg (14kpl).

and no tow bar, whilst the GE also had the large-capacity compartment plus an air tank, presumably intended for tyre inflation. For 1933, the range was expanded to include the GDT, which had the large-capacity rear compartment plus the tow bar. The GE was dropped in 1940, and the GD and GDT were discontinued in 1942. By 1964, just one model was being offered, under the designation GE not the old Model GE, but a standard 'Servi-Car' without tow bar. The Model GE remained in the company's catalogue until the end of 1973.

Throughout the 42-year production life of the vehicle, power was provided by the trusty 737cc (45cu.in) side-valve V-twin engine. For the years 1932 to 1935, it was the R Series, the engine which had been introduced in 1929 for the Model D; from 1936 subsequent vehicles were fitted with the W Series engine.

Left: The 'Servi-Car' was also widely used by police departments across the country for duties such as parking control. Throughout the 42-year life of the vehicle, power was provided by the trusty 737cc (45cu.in) side-valve V-twin engine. The glass fibre rear box identifies this as a late model. (DK)

Below left: In 1940, the 'Servi-Car' was used as a basis for this three-seat 3x2 'field car'. Designated Model TA, the normal rear locker is replaced by a small bench seat and there were disc wheels. The prototype was powered by the 999cc (61cu. in) 'Knucklehead' engine, driving the rear wheels via a propeller shaft, but a single example was modified by boring the engine out to 1130cc (69cu.in). (FC)

This is the unit which also powered thousands of military WLAs during World War Two. Power from the engine was transmitted to the rear axle via a three-speed gearbox (with reverse) and an open chain driving a large sprocket in the differential housing. This housing also carried a central drum brake, intended to provide equal braking effort on the two rear wheels.

In appearance, the vehicle changed little over the years, the most noticeable change being the adoption of the overall styling of the Model E in 1937. Earlier visual changes had included the use of straight grab bars on the rear compartment in 1934, rather than the original curly art-deco shape. A shorter more rectangular rear box was fitted on non-tow bar equipped variants from 1935.

The W Series engine which replaced the earlier R Series in 1936 had the same bore and stroke as the old model, but significant improvements were made internally and power output was increased. At the same time, the opportunity was taken to fit separate brakes to each rear wheel. Also a new instrument panel was fitted to the tank, with a speedometer, oil-pressure gauge, ammeter, ignition switch and speedometer light switch. Larger hubcaps became a fitment.

A considerable number of detailed engineering changes were made in the years 1937 and 1938 and, for 1939 the rear box was made larger. A chromium-plated rear bumper was

PRODUCTION AND PRICES, ALL G SERIES 'SERVI-CAR' MODELS

Date	Number	Retail price	Date	Number	Retail price	Date	Number	Retail price
1932	260	$450	1946	1444	$582-593	1960	707	$1500-1530
1933	182	n/a	1947	2177	$695-710	1961	628	$1525-1555
1934	546	$415-485	1948	1778	$740-755	1962	703	$1525-1555
1935	567	$425-495	1949	1039	$845-860	1963	n/a	$1550-1590
1936	648	$425-495	1950	1003	$845-860	1964	725	$1628
1937	816	$500-570	1951	1410	$1080-1095	1965	625	n/a
1938	625	$515-530	1952	1047	$1160-1175	1966	625	n/a
1939	650	$515-530	1953	1146	$1175-1190	1967	600	$1930
1940	908	$515-530	1954	1397	$1225-1240	1968	600	$1930
1941	1159	$515-530	1955	1041	$1225-1240	1969	475	$2065
1942	399	$510-525	1956	1203	$1225-1240	1970	494	n/a
1943	135	$500-515	1957	1192	$1352-1367	1971	500	n/a
1944	57	$500-515	1958	926	$1450-1465	1972	400	n/a
1945	86	$568-580	1959	812	$1470-1500	1973	425	n/a

Total number produced, around 32,160, although the exact production figure for 1963 is not known.

Introduced in 1936, the Model W replaced the R series although it continued to be fitted with the 737cc (45cu.in) side-valve V-twin engine. The large-section tyres, teardrop tank, integrated instrument panel and curved mudguards were typical of two decades of Harley-Davidson styling. (DK)

made available as an option. Detailed changes continued throughout 1940 and 1941. Few modifications were made during the latter years of the war, the most notable being the rationalisation of the range to just two models in 1942, the G and the GA, both with the same size rear compartment.

In 1941, the company supplied the US Army with four GA 'Servi-Cars', one of which (registered USA 65447) was fitted with a General Electric (GE) radio, presumably as an experiment in mobile communications, perhaps for use in convoy escort work or as a forward observation post for artillery. Military modifications were probably confined to the use of blackout lighting and the familiar all-over drab green paint finish.

Full-scale civilian production resumed in 1947, when the most significant change was to the gear-shift pattern. Chrome-plated parts started to return, ousting the utility appearance of the war years. A motorcar-type clutch pedal was fitted in 1948.

The US Army purchased more 'Servi-Cars' in 1950, for use by Military Police and as convoy escort and messenger vehicles. Although generally similar to civilian machines of the same period, the tricycles were fitted with additional hazard lights. All were painted olive drab.

The most significant 'civilian' change that year was made to the shape of the front mudguard. In 1951 bigger changes were made with the adoption of hydraulic brakes and five-bolt one-piece disc wheels, the latter replacing the motorcycle-type spoked wheels.

The year 1958 saw the adoption of the 'Hydra-Glide' front forks, brakes and axle. Changes made during the next few years were largely cosmetic, but an electric starter appeared for the first time in 1964. The electrical system was upgraded to 12V using a two-brush generator. This generator was replaced by an alternator and rectifier for 1966.

In 1967 the old-style metal storage box was replaced by a fibreglass unit, which incorporated moulded-in rear mudguards. This unit was moulded at Harley-Davidson's Tomahawk boat plant.

During the last few years of the vehicle's production life, such changes as were made were minimal but, surprisingly, six-bolt wheels were adopted in 1973 along with hydraulic disc brakes. Sales had scarcely exceeded 500 a year since 1969.

The last year of the 'Servi-Car', 1973, ended what had been a very successful production run.

MODEL R

The Model R was announced at the end of 1931 for the 1932 model year. It was a development of the first of the company's iconic 737cc (45cu.in) side-valve V-twins, the Model D of 1929, and was part of a model line which eventually culminated in the most celebrated of all Harley-Davidson's military V-twins, the WLA.

Above: Officers of the Minnesota Police Department mounted on Model V motorcycles. The big 1,213cc (74cu.in) side-valve V-twin engine boasted a 36bhp power output. (DA)

With its lightweight engine-hugging frame, the Model D might have looked the business but, in truth, it was no great shakes, production actually having to be suspended at one point to redesign certain features. But within three years, with improvements such as aluminium pistons, stronger valve springs, a new crankcase, larger flywheel, better lubrication,

Technical specification

Models R, RS, RL, RLD.

Engine:
737cc (45cu.in) Harley-Davidson '45'; two cylinders in 45° 'V' formation; bore and stroke, 2.8in x 3.8 in (70mm x 97mm); side valves; dry sump; air cooled; power output, 19bhp at 4600rpm.

Transmission:
3F; hand gear-change; multi-plate dry clutch; duplex primary roller-chain running in closed casing; exposed roller-chain drive to rear wheel; primary and secondary chains on opposite sides of the engine.

Suspension:
parallelogram leading-link steel I-beam front forks with twin coil springs; adjustable suspension geometry; solid rear forks.

Brakes:
drum brakes front and rear; mechanically-operated by rod and cable; front and rear.

Tyre size:
3.50-18, same size front and rear.

Construction:
cycle type steel-tube frame.

Electrical system:
6V battery.

Dimensions
Length, 86in (2.2m); *width*, 37in (.94m); *height*, n/a.
Wheelbase, 57.5in (1.5m).
Ground clearance, 4in (102mm).
Unladen weight, 390lb (177kg).

Performance
Maximum allowable speed, 70mph (113kph).
Range of action, n/a.
Average fuel consumption, n/a.

Comprehensive performance and dimensional data was not always available for militarised civilian models.

and a redesigned, strengthened frame, it had evolved into the highly-creditable Model R.

Even in its improved form, the 737cc (45cu.in) V-twin engine was little more than two 345cc (21cu.in) single-cylinder barrels with removable Ricardo heads, such had been used for the Models A and B dating back to 1926, assembled onto a common crankcase. Yet, with the side valves located in the cylinder castings, and even allowing for the air spaces between the cylinders and the exhaust ports, it was far cheaper to manufacture than the complex inlet-over-exhaust engines – the so-called 'F-heads' – which had gone before and, at the same time, offered better performance and greater reliability. The frame down-tube was also redesigned to accommodate a larger, horizontally-mounted generator, the same as that fitted to the flagship 1,213cc (74cu.in) models.

From the outset, the new motorcycle was offered in a range of four models, all of them featuring a three-speed transmission.

The Model R was the entry level, a low-compression engined solo machine priced at just $295; the RS used the same engine but incorporated sidecar gearing and was also priced at $295. The RL had magnesium-alloy pistons manufacture by Dow Metal and was fitted with medium-compression heads, and again was just $295; whilst the $310 Model RLD special sport was a high-performance solo machine with high-compression heads. Total production for 1932 amounted to 1,247 units, the majority of which were of the medium performance RL.

The standard single-seat sidecar for the Model R, regardless of year of manufacture, was the Model LS.

The standard models continued virtually unchanged for 1933, with prices of $280 and $290, but the range was expanded to include the Models RE, RLE and RLDE, fitted with magnesium-alloy pistons. The depression was taking its toll with the lack of buyers and the shortage of development money which meant that, aside from the so-called 'ride control' feature – a slotted link on the front forks which allowed adjustment of the suspension geometry whilst on the move – there were few modifications made to the models. Production stood at just 544 for the year.

Low-expansion alloy pistons were adopted across the range in 1934, which saw the Models RE, RLE and RLDE deleted;

Right: The Model E of 1936 featured the overhead-valve 'Knucklehead' engine, so called because the valve covers resembled knuckles. Power output was 40bhp from 999cc (61cu.in). This was also the first Harley-Davidson to feature a recirculating lubrication system. Note the adjustable front-suspension. (DC/BVMM)

new 'X' suffix models (RX, RLX, RLDX and RSX) were produced for export to Germany. Modifications introduced for the year included a new-type oil pump, improvements to the total-loss lubrication system, and the adoption of an improved 12-spring clutch; visually, the motorcycles benefited from new-style mudguards. The prices remained at $280 and $290, with some 1,735 machines sold; although it should be noted that 1934 models remained on sale for 16 months, from the autumn of 1933.

For 1935, the constant-mesh gearbox of the Model G 'Servi-Car' was adopted, together with straight-bore cylinders and Lynite T-slot pistons, quick-release wheels, improved brakes and a new toolbox. The prices were raised to $295 and $305, with production up to a far more respectable 2,020 machines, including 50 examples of the Model RSR for export to Japan and 29 examples of the RLDR competition special, which was priced at $322.

The range was unchanged for 1936, although this was the last year of production for the Model R it being replaced by the improved W the following year. Changes for the year included improved engine cooling arrangements, redesigned combustion chambers, a new larger-diameter Y-shaped inlet manifold which improved performance, and thicker brake linings. Production totalled 1,871 examples of the standard models, plus 30 of the RSR for the Japanese market, and 79 competition RLDRs. Prices were $295 for the standard models and $320 for the RLDR.

Total production of all R series models stood at 7,526, but the Models R and RL were the only motorcycles from the series to see any military service, the US Army taking delivery of examples of the model in 1932, with some RLs following in 1934 and 1935. However, there is no evidence that these machines were anything other than standard civilian types.

Technical specification

Models ES, ELA, ELC.

Classification:
standard.

Engine:
999cc (61cu.in) Harley-Davidson '61'; two cylinders in 42° 'V' formation; bore and stroke, 3.3in x 3.5in (84mm x 89mm); overhead valves; dry sump; air cooled; power output, 40–45bhp at 4800rpm.

Transmission:
4F; hand gear-change; multi-plate dry clutch; duplex primary roller-chain running in closed casing; exposed roller-chain drive to rear wheel; primary and secondary chains on left-hand side of the engine.

Suspension:
parallelogram leading-link steel-tube front forks with single coil spring, friction damped; solid rear forks.

Brakes:
drum brakes; front and rear (including sidecar); mechanically operated.

Tyre size:
4.50-18 (5.00-16 optional from 1940), same size front and rear.

Construction:
duplex steel-tube frame.

Electrical system:
6V battery.

Dimensions
(with standard sidecar)
Length, 95.5in (2.4m);
width, 69in (1.8m);
height, 42.5in (1.10m).
Wheelbase, 59.5in (1.5m).
Ground clearance, 4.1in (104mm).
Unladen weight, 515lb (234kg).

Performance
Maximum allowable speed, 95mph to 100mph (153kph to 161kph) (solo); 55mph (89kph) (with sidecar). Range of action, 112 miles (180km). Average fuel consumption, 38mpg (13.5kpl).

MODEL E

In 1936, Harley-Davidson launched the Model E, fitted with a powerful 999cc (61cu.in) overhead-valve engine which was quickly dubbed the 'Knucklehead' for the shape of the valve covers. These resembled clenched knuckles. Designed by William S. Harley and Lothar A. Doerner, and inheriting little more than the mudguards and generator from the Model V, which it replaced, this was an all-new machine with a brand-new frame. At a launch price of $380, just $40 more than the Model V, the E was a success from the outset. Over 1,800 were shipped in the first year of production.

For the first two years, the range comprised of the Model E, a medium-compression solo machine, the Model ES, which was the sidecar equivalent and the Model EL 'Special Sport', a solo machine with high-compression heads and a 40bhp power output; all three models incorporated a four-speed

Above: The new 'Knucklehead' engine did not replace the side-valve unit which continued to be fitted in the Models W and U (shown), the latter using the 1,213cc (74cu.in) unit. (DA)

transmission. Oil for the dry-sump motor was carried in a separate U-shaped tank located behind the engine and was fed to the moving parts by a single check-valve pump. There were folding footboards and interchangeable (front to back) wheels. A built-in instrument panel was mounted on the distinctive tear-drop fuel tank.

The Model E was not without teething troubles and, during the first year, the frame was redesigned to prevent cracking. Also there were changes to the oil tank, the kickstarter gearing and the cylinder heads.

The range remained unchanged for 1937 but the frame was further reinforced and the sidecar mounts were redesigned. Rear brake diameter was also increased. The optional ride-control system was offered; fitted to the front forks, this allowed the rider to alter the suspension geometry on the move. The price increased to $435 and production for the year stood at 2,020 units.

The base Model E was dropped from the range in 1938, leaving just the ES and the EL. For the first time, the valve gear was completely enclosed, which meant that the road and rider no longer enjoyed the dubious benefits of the total-loss lubrication system. This new valve gear could also be retro-fitted to earlier machines. Other changes included further strengthening of the frame, together with a redesigned steering head, improvements to the clutch and transmission. Higher-type handlebars were also fitted. Some 2,478 examples were sold at a price of $435.

There were more detail changes for 1939, and this was the first year in which the US Army specified a militarised version of the sidecar Model ES. This appears to have been confusingly – or erroneously – described by the US Ordnance Department as the Model ELA, rather than ESA which would have been more logical. The 'A' suffix, as before, denoting that this was an 'army' model. The machines were supplied in very small numbers and were used for convoy escort work, messenger duties also naval shore and base patrols.

Changes from the civilian machine included a utility finish, increased mudguard clearance, low-compression cylinder heads, an oil-bath air cleaner, lower gear ratios and standard-type military lighting fittings. The latter probably included the fitting of blackout lighting.

The price of the ES and EL remained at $435 for 1939, and production of all E series models stood at 2,909 for the year.

During 1940, some 4,069 examples were produced at a price of $430 each; changes were strictly engineering and included up-rated crankshaft main bearings and a new constant-mesh transmission. A heavier flywheel was adopted for 1941, together with an improved clutch. The Model ELA was now standardised by the US Army. The price was reduced to $425 and production totalled 2,541 examples.

A similar model to the ELA was produced for the Canadian Army in 1941/42, described as the ELC, differing in detail only from its US Army counterpart; one example, fitted with a left-hand LLE sidecar was delivered to the British War Office in 1941 for evaluation, but the type was not adopted.

The Model ES was dropped in 1942 and the E reintroduced. This meant that the civilian range now comprised the high-compression EL and the medium-compression E, both priced at $425. The military models included the ELA and the ELC. Production totalled 792 for the year, just 53 of those machines built were military models.

Models E and EL remained in production for 1943, at the same price of $425, with production totalling just 158. The sidecar Model ES was reinstated for 1944, which probably indicates that the special 'Army' model was no longer in production. The price for 1944 was also unchanged and just 296 examples were built.

Aluminium cylinder heads were offered as an option in 1945, but there was no more military production of the Model E. The civilian range was unchanged, comprising Models E, ES and EL, priced at $463, with 680 machines constructed. Civilian production got back into full swing the following year, when the most significant change was the mid-year introduction of offset forks. The price was unchanged but production surged to 2,342. The gear-shifter gate pattern was revised in 1947, and the price of the three models was up to $590; production stood at 4,354.

The new 'Panhead' engine was adopted in 1948, featuring hydraulic valve-lifters and aluminium cylinder heads. This was fitted into a redesigned frame and the price increased to $635, with 4,519 machines produced. However, this was strictly an interim model, made up of a hybrid of the old Model E with the new engine. It was replaced by the much-improved Model E 'Hydra-Glide' in 1949, which remained in production for another eight years. The 'Panhead' engine was to remain in production until 1966.

The standard single-passenger sidecar throughout the production run was the Model LE; the LLE was similar but designed for fitting to the left-hand side of the motorcycle frame. Total production of the Model E between 1936 and 1948 was 28,958.

World War Two

Before the advent of the ubiquitous Jeep, the design of which did not start until mid-1940, the US Army envisaged that motorcycles would be widely used in convoy escort, reconnaissance and despatch rider duties. Although the Jeep changed all this; nevertheless the US government purchased thousands of motorcycles during the years 1941 to 1945. Best known of these was the Harley-Davidson WLA.

CHAPTER 4 WORLD WAR TWO

When the US entered the war in December 1941, the Department of Defense started to purchase motorcycles from both Harley-Davidson and Indian. Harley's major contribution was the 737cc (45cu.in) WLA, a military special derived from the civilian WL of 1937, which, in turn, was based on the sport solo Model DLD of 1930. A variant was also built for the Canadian Army known as the WLC, and a small number of these were used by the British Royal Air Force.

Several reputable histories of Harley-Davidson assert that soon after the outbreak of World War Two, both the company and Indian received orders for 500 – some claim 5,000 – heavy solo machines from the British Ministry of Supply (MoS) anxious to supplement a shortage of British-built machines. Although there is certainly documentary evidence of Indian having supplied a total of more than 5,760 machines of various types to the MoS before the war ended, the same documents record just a handful of Harley-Davidsons received during the same period. Nevertheless, many writers insist that large numbers of Harley-Davidsons were supplied to Britain under the provisions of the 1941 Lend-Lease Act.

When the US entered the war in December 1941, the Department of Defense (DoD) placed a series of major contracts with Harley-Davidson. The company's major contribution to the Allied armies was the 737cc (45cu.in) WLA – sometimes described as the 'Liberator' – a militarised version of the civilian model WL of 1937, which, in turn, was based on the sport solo Model DLD of 1930. The 'A' suffix to the model number indicated that this was a special 'Army'

model. A designated model, the WLC, was also built for the Canadian Army. A small number of these were supplied to the Royal Air Force (RAF). The 'standardised' version of this machine was the 42-WLA, produced between September 1941 and August 1945.

Although some 80,000 WLAs were produced, this was not the only Harley-Davidson motorcycle supplied to the US Army during this period, although it was certainly the most numerous. Starting in 1944, the company also supplied small quantities of the more-powerful Models ELA, FS, UA, UH and US, in solo and combination form. As well as the

Previous pages: November 1944. The road sign shows that this US soldier of the 315th Engineer Battalion, 90th Infantry Division, has entered Hitler's Germany. The heavily laden WLA – sometimes described as the 'Liberator' – probably carries everything he needs for his day-to-day survival, his rifle, entrenching tool and bedroll. The rubber suit has been liberated from a captured German. (NA)

Right: Whilst the WLA was the most numerous Harley-Davidson in military service, the big Models E and U were both used in solo and sidecar form, particularly by the US Navy. The Model U, shown, was effectively an E with the 1,213cc (74cu.in) side-valve engine. (USQM)

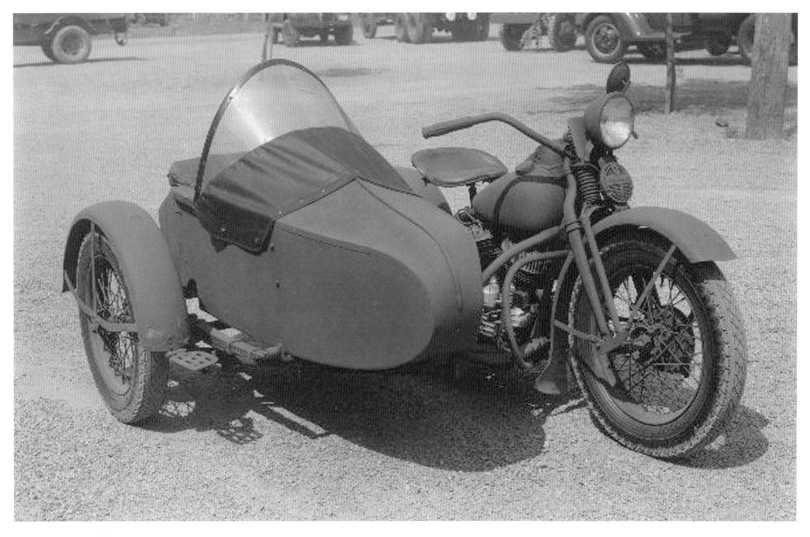

US Army, both the US Navy and the US Marine Corps used these machines.

Other models produced for the military included the BMW-inspired, shaft-drive Model XA which was produced between 1941 and 1943 supposedly for use in the North African desert. Only 1,011 Model Xs were built. The XAS was a combination outfit fitted with a driven sidecar wheel, but it is possible that just one example was constructed. Both the XA and the XAS were powered by new horizontal flat-twin cylinder engine of 739cc (45cu.in). The US Army also purchased four examples of the three-wheeled 'Servi-Car', designated GA. The 'Servi-Car' first appeared in 1932 and ultimately enjoyed the longest production run of any Harley-Davidson model, used the V-twin 737cc (45cu.in) side-valve engine which had been launched in 1929.

Almost 1,600 Model US twins, with left-hand-mounted sidecars, were supplied under Lend-Lease to British forces in South Africa via the British Supply Council in 1942. During 1941 to 1942 Model ELC and two WLCs were also supplied to the British for evaluation.

All civilian Harley-Davidson production ceased on 9 February 1942, and by August of that year production stood at 750 machines per week, all intended for the military or other government agencies. The Service School also reverted to the original role and was, once again, used by the US Army Quartermaster Corps as a training facility for military mechanics.

William Herbert Davidson, the son of William A. Davidson, had taken on the role of President of the company following the death of Walter Davidson in 1942 at the age of 66. The

company suffered a further blow when William Harley died in 1943; his duties as Chief Engineer were taken over by William Ottway Snr and subsequently by his son, William Ottway Jnr. During this period, all Harley-Davidson motorcycles were supplied on the same pricing basis – cost plus 10%, which resulted in a profit margin of 6%; the average price of a WLA during the war was $380.

The company received two, perhaps four, Army-Navy 'E' awards for excellent service, in 1943 and 1945. By the time the war came to an end, Harley-Davidson had supplied Allied forces with more than 88,000 motorcycles. Official US figures claim that two-thirds of these motorcycles were 'Lend-Lease' to the Allies. Military production ceased in early 1945 and it is rumoured that the US government failed to honour its commitment for the cost of spare parts, and that outstanding contracts for 15,000 machines were cancelled.

MODEL U

Launched in 1937 as a replacement for the Model V, the side-valve Model U 'big twin' was offered with a choice of either a 1,213cc (74cu.in) engine, or a high-performance 1,311cc (80cu.in) unit. The engine was an all-new dry-sump design, echoing the changes and improvements – particularly to the

Above: Launched in 1937 as a replacement for the Model V, the side-valve Model U 'big twin' was offered with a choice of either a 1,213cc (74cu.in) engine, or a high-performance 1,311cc (80cu.in) unit. The range was rationalised at the end of 1941, when the Model UA was classified as 'standard' by the US military with the 1,213cc (74cu.in) engine. The machine's apparent scarcity in restored form simply reflects the small numbers originally procured. (DC/BVMM)

Right: The ubiquitous Harley-Davidson Model WLA. (DC/BVMM)

Above: The 1,213cc (74cu.in) Harley-Davidson 74 engine as fitted in the Model U. The 1,311cc (80cu.in) Harley-Davidson 80 was also fitted in this model. (DC/BVMM)

lubrication system – which had been made to the overhead-valve power unit first fitted to the Model E.

Initially comprising six models, the range included three machines fitted with the 1,213cc (74cu.in) engine, and three with the larger 1,311cc (80cu.in) unit. Of the smaller engined motorcycles, the Model U was for solo use and had medium-compression cylinder heads, the similar Model US was intended to be fitted with a sidecar and featured lower gearing to suit this role. The UL was a 'sporty' solo machine fitted with high-compression heads. The UH, USH and ULH offered the same range of features, respectively, but utilised

the 1,311cc (80cu.in) engine. Just one of these high-performance machines was supplied for military service. Regardless of the individual model, the engine was linked to a four-speed transmission derived from that used on the Model E, whilst the frame was also similar to that designed for the Model E. Harley-Davidson's optional ride-control system was available for the front forks.

Technical specification

Models U, UA, UH, UL, ULH, US, USH.

Engine:
1,213cc (74cu.in) or 1,311cc (80cu.in) Harley-Davidson '74' or '80'; two cylinders in 45° 'V' formation; bore and stroke, 3.4in x 4.0in (87mm x 102mm), or 3.4in x 4.25in (87mm x 108mm); side valves; dry sump; air cooled; power output, 33–37bhp at 4,600rpm.

Transmission:
3F; hand gear-change; multi-plate dry clutch; duplex primary roller-chain running in closed casing; exposed roller-chain drive to rear wheel; primary and secondary chains on left-hand side of motor.

Suspension:
parallelogram leading-link steel-tube front forks with twin coil springs; solid rear forks.

Brakes:
mechanically operated drum brakes; front and rear.

Tyre size:
4.50-18, or 5.50-16, same size front and rear.

Construction:
duplex steel-tube frame; wishbone-type downtube for 1948.

Electrical system:
6V battery.

Dimensions
Length, 96in (2.4m); *width*, 69in (1.8m); *height* (with windscreen), 42.5in (1.10m).
Wheelbase, 59.5in (1.5m).
Ground clearance, 4.75in (121mm).
Unladen weight, 850lb (386kg).

Performance
Maximum allowable speed, 55mph (88kph).
Range of action, 112 miles (180km).
Average fuel consumption, 32mpg (11kpl)).

Launch price was $395 or $415, according to the engine option, and a total of 6,651 machines was sold in the first year.

The standard right-hand single-passenger sidecar throughout the production run was the Model LE; the left-hand mount equivalent was the LLE.

For 1938, the frame was reinforced, and a higher handlebar position was adopted to improve riding comfort. Both the clutch and transmission were also reinforced. The range remained unchanged with six models and prices were held at $395 and $415. Total production amounted to 2,625.

The six models also remained in the catalogue for 1939, although the range was briefly expanded for 1939 and 1940 to include the Model UMG, a 1,213cc (74cu.in) engined machine fitted with a Bosch magneto ignition system. A large number of engineering changes were made, including the option of specifying a revised transmission. This included a sliding-type gears for easier changes between second and third. Prices were held at the 1937 figures and production for the year stood at 3,235 units.

A number of examples of the civilian Model UL were purchased by the US Army between 1938 and 1939, fitted with the standard single-passenger Model LE sidecar. The motorcycle and sidecar were fitted with a windscreen and, although the outfits were finished in gloss olive green, there were no military modifications. Other military experiments during 1939 and 1940 included a civilian Model UL fitted with a special machine-gun-mounted sidecar. This was a water-cooled .30 calibre Browning M1917A1 on what appears to be a standard ground-mount tripod fitted with an elevating anti-aircraft attachment allowing the gun to achieve a higher trajectory. A curved armoured shield was fitted to the single-seat sidecar. An angled armoured shield with a small windscreen was also fitted to protect the rider. There does not appear to have been any series production, almost certainly because the Jeep was far more effective in this type of role.

The US Army also purchased a number of civilian Model U solo machines in 1939 before specifying a militarised version of the sidecar Model US, under the designation UA. The first contract (QM-7096) called for 335 machines, with a further 509 following in 1940 under contracts QM-7518 and 7737. Changes from the civilian specification included high-clearance mudguards, blackout lighting, overall olive drab paint finish, revised gearing and fire extinguisher. The sidecar was the standard civilian type Model LE, with or without windscreen as specified in the contract.

Improvements were also minor for 1940, the most notable being larger main bearings in the engine and interconnected fuel tanks. Prices were reduced by $10 for the 1,213cc (74cu.in) engined variants, and $5 for the 1,311cc (80cu.in) engines. Total production for the year was 2,910.

The crankcase, oil pump and clutch were redesigned for 1941 and the neck angle on the frame was altered to 29°. Total production amounted to 4,145 machines but, of course, this was the first year in which civilian motorcycle production was suspended. A single example of the Model UH solo machine was supplied to the US Army under contract QM-9043 (registration number USA 65446). It was fitted with RCA radio equipment presumably for trialling the possibility of adopting motorcycles for the communications role. Again, the availability of the Jeep probably brought this experiment to an end.

The range was rationalised at the end of 1941, when the Model UA was classified as 'standard' by the US Army. Alongside the military UA, only the 1,213cc (74cu.in) engined Models U, UL and US remained in production. The larger-engined models having been dropped to avoid competing with the overhead-valve 1,213cc (74cu.in) Model F which had been introduced that year. Such changes as were made were relatively minor, and for 1942, just 467 examples were sold: the number increased to 1,819 in 1943. A total of 1,315 were part of an order for some 1,597 examples of the Model US sidecar outfit (fitted with an LLE sidecar) which were supplied to South Africa through the British Supply Council (contract LL-NDS-105.A). The price remained at $385.

Production fell back in 1944, with 1,152 examples sold, again at a price of $385. The only noteworthy change being the adoption of synthetic rubber tyres.

Civilian production restarted in 1945, with a total of 1,285 machines being sold at an increased price of $427. For the first time, aluminium cylinder heads were offered as an option. Further modest changes were made in 1946, including the adoption of a 30° neck angle on the frame. Although the Model U must have clearly been reaching the end of its life, demand was such that 3,522 were sold, with the price held at $427 per unit.

A new gear-shift pattern was adopted for 1947, along with a number of cosmetic and detailed changes. Chrome-plated items were fitted for the first time since the war. Although the price increased to $545 a total of 2,932 were sold.

During 1948, the last year of production for the Model U, the frame was redesigned to incorporate a wishbone-type downtube, steering lock and crash bars. Sales dropped by almost 600 machines to 2,377 whilst the price rose to $590.

The following year the Model U was replaced by the Model F 'Hydra-Glide', a thoroughly modern machine with fitted hydraulic front forks.

Total sales of all variants of the Model U during 12 years in production was 33,129.

MODEL W

The Model W first appeared in 1937 to replace the ageing Model R. It was powered by an updated version of the iconic 737cc (45cu.in) side-valve V-twin, and adopted the more modern external styling of the Model E. Major changes to the engine included the adoption of roller bearings, and the use of the dry-sump lubrication system, which had been introduced for the 999cc (61cu.in) models in 1936. Ride-control system was also fitted. Other improvements included the use of automatic primary-chain lubrication and big, twin fuel tanks, mounted each side of the frame top tube which also provided a handy mount for the instrument panel.

As launched, the standard range comprised five models. The Model W was a solo machine fitted with low-compression heads with the WS as the sidecar equivalent. The WL was a solo sport machine with high-compression heads and the WLD was fitted with extra-high compression heads. The WLDR – the 'R' indicating a racing model – was described as a 'competition special'. There was also a Model WSR intended for export to Japan. All were fitted with a three-speed transmission. The launch price was $355, except for the WLDR which attracted a $25 premium. Sales for the first year stood at 2,031.

Top right: Although the WLA was at home anywhere, it was by no means an off-road machine – the poor ground clearance tending to militate against arduous off-road riding. However, it had plenty of torque and was extremely reliable. (SANMMH)

Right: Line-up of South African WLAs. (SANMMH)

Above: The Harley-Davidson Model U can be easily identified from the WLA by smaller diameter wheels. (SANMMH)

The standard sidecar for the Model W was the Model LS until this was discontinued in 1948. The LS was replaced by the LE, which was suitable for use across the entire Harley-Davidson range of motorcycles.

Changes for 1938 and 1939 were minor, although there were improvements to the clutch and transmission in 1938, paralleling those which had been made to the 'big twins'. The ride-control system was also changed to improve ride comfort. The first military WLA appeared in 1939, with two prototype models being shipped to Fort Knox, Kentucky for trials. Prices remained at $355 and $380, with sales for the two years totalling 1,399 and 1,414 units, respectively.

Aluminium cylinder heads were adopted for Models WLD and WLDR in 1940, these were designed with improved cooling fins and changes to the carburettor. Further changes were made to the design of the transmission and also to the front forks across the complete range. Total sales for the year amounted to 1,864, with prices at $350 for the W, WS and WL with $365 for the WLD and $395 for the WLDR.

Above: A Model US with left-hand sidecar being used to collect vital rations. The South African rider appears to be a civilian. (SANMMH)

The frame was redesigned in 1941 to accept a new transmission. Further improvements were made to the clutch and braking systems and 16in wheels were adopted as standard. The range was rationalised by deleting the base Model W and re-designating the sidecar model as WLS. The price of the WLDR was reduced to $385 but other prices were held at 1940 levels; total sales stood at 4,939 units. A new stripped-down racing model was introduced, designated WR.

Civilian production more-or-less ceased in 1942, with the WLDR and WR being removed from the catalogue. Changes were minimal and production was concentrated on military machines; just 142 WLs and 133 WLDRs were produced with showroom sticker prices standing at $350 and $365, respectively.

There was no further production by Harley-Davidson of civilian W models until 1945, when the WL was reintroduced. A total of 1,357 examples were sold, at a price of $395. Aluminium cylinder heads were offered as an option from 1946, under the designation WL-SP, at a $7 price premium.

The WL was joined by the WLS 'sidecar twin' in 1948; the WR Racer was also reintroduced. In 1951, the range was expanded further by the announcement of a 'Tourist Trophy' racer under the designation WRTT. However, by 1952, the last year of production, the only model available was the WLS.

Changes were minimal and largely cosmetic during these last years, with chrome-plated parts starting to be fitted in 1947. Continual cosmetic changes were made to seats, badging, lights, and paintwork, and the adoption of 'airflow' mudguards in 1951. The most noticeable change was probably the adoption of a fixed-jet Linkert carburettor.

The machine continued to sell well, with 4,410 produced in 1946, 3,338 in 1947, 2,416 in 1948, and 2,725 in 1949. By 1950, the Model W was beginning to look a little dated – hydraulic front forks, for example were never fitted on this model – and sales dropped to 1,123. There was a further fall to 1,068 in 1951. During this time, the price rose steadily, from $490 in 1946 rising by 50% to $730 during the last year of production. Total production of W series models (excluding military WLA and WLC) stood at 26,960 by the time the range was superseded by the new Model K in 1952.

Left: Fourth from the left is a lone Harley WLA in a line-up of motorcycles in South African Army service. (SANMMH)

Below: South African Army Commandos mounted on Harley-Davidsons. Note the different styles of tin helmets worn and all are armed with British-manufactured Lee-Enfield .303 rifles. (SANMMH)

Left: South African motorcycle troops. Among the line-up are two Harley-Davidson Model Us; the rest are of British origin. (SANMMH)

Right: US Army despatch rider practising cross-country riding on a WLA. The rider is wearing a respirator in this 1939 training photograph. (USQM)

Below: In 1942, around 1,600 Model Us with left-hand sidecars, were supplied under the Lend-Lease programme to British forces in South Africa via the British Supply Council. (SANMMH)

Left: The skirted mudguards make this look like a militarised Model WL, probably of 1940. Compared to a British-built motorcycle of World War Two the Harley-Davidson was heavy and old fashioned, although certainly not lacking in power or reliability. (SANMMH)

Right: A factory fresh Harley-Davidson WLC ready for delivery to the Canadian Army. In the background are Windsor carriers built by Ford of Canada. (NAC)

Below: Escort riders of the Australian Army mounted on Harley-Davidson WLAs. (NAA)

Only the WL appears to have seen any military service, the US Army taking delivery of small numbers in 1937, 1939 and 1945, the latter alongside the specialised WLA. The WLA, as with the military WL was classified as 'standard'. These were more-or-less standard civilian machines, but one interesting variation involved the use of 4.00-18 wheels and tyres on the 1945 models. Although these would have been standard in 1937, the smaller 16in (41cm) wheels not becoming a fitment

until 1941, the use on machines built in 1945 was presumably to provide commonality with the WLA.

The sidecar-equipped Model WLS was also trialled by the Danish Army in 1939, but was deemed unsuitable on account of size and weight.

MODELS WLA, WLC

With a possible total production of more than 78,000 machines, the Model WLA is the most numerous, and is certainly best known, of the military Harley-Davidsons. Although it is actually nothing more than a militarised Model WL. The first incarnation of the WLA was found in a pair of modified WLs supplied to the US Army in 1939 for trials. With few changes, production of the militarised WLA started in March of the following year with the company maintaining a prodigious rate of output, sometimes reaching 750 machines a week. In recognition of this, Harley-Davidson received an unprecedented two – indeed, some say, four – Army-Navy 'E' awards for excellence.

Registered USA 61995 and USA 61996, the two prototypes for what was to become the WLA were supplied to the US Army in August 1939 under contract QM-7238 which was actually dated 1940, but presumably was issued after the event. It is probable that the Army had originally wanted a purpose-designed military 500cc (30cu.in) machine which could be used for Military Police, convoy escort, despatch rider and reconnaissance duties. The military requested design submissions from Harley-Davidson, Indian and GM-Delco. Harley-Davidson had nothing available with a suitable engine, and was not prepared to produce a 'special' for the Army. A compromise was agreed upon whereby the company would provide the 737cc (45cu.in) Model WL which had been modified to be more suited for military service.

Finished in a gloss olive green paint, the two Harley-Davidson prototypes were sent to Fort Knox, Kentucky (home of the US Cavalry) and to Camp Holabird, Maryland.

Technical specification

Models W, WL, WLS, WLD, WLDR.

Engine:
737cc (45cu.in) Harley-Davidson '45'; two cylinders in 45° 'V' formation; bore and stroke, 2.8in x 3.9in (70mm x 98mm); side valves; air cooled; dry sump; power output, 23bhp at 4,600rpm; torque, 27.5 lbf/ft at 4,000rpm.

Transmission:
3F (1937-1940), 4F (1940-1952); hand gear-change; multi-plate dry clutch; duplex primary roller-chain running in closed casing; exposed roller-chain drive to rear wheel; primary and secondary chains on opposite sides of motor.

Suspension:
parallelogram leading-link steel-tube front forks with twin coil springs; adjustable suspension geometry; solid rear forks.

Brakes:
mechanically operated drum brakes; front and rear.

Tyre size:
4.00-18 (1937–1941), 5.00-16 (optional for 1940, standard for 1941–1952), same size front and rear.

Construction:
cycle type steel-tube frame.

Electrical system:
6V battery.

Dimensions
Length, 88in (2.24m); *width*, 36in (91cm); *height*, 41in (1.04m). *Wheelbase*, 57.5in (1.46m). *Ground clearance*, 4.5in (114mm). *Unladen weight*, 477lb (216kg).

Performance
Maximum allowable speed, 70mph (113kph). Range of action, 125 miles (201km). Average fuel consumption, 40mpg (14kpl).

Right: Photographed in July 1944, despatch rider Private Robert J. Vance of Portland, Oregon was attached to an armoured unit in France and was delivering messages to the front line. The motorcycle is a typical wartime WLA, albeit with leg guards. (NA)

In its specification, the Army was most insistent that the motorcycles should not overheat when used for slow-speed convoy and escort work. For this reason, the 737cc (45cu.in) side-valve V-twin engine of the WL was downrated reducing the compression ratio to 5:1 by using aluminium cylinder heads. The company's engineers also cast larger-section cooling fins in the cylinder block, as well as making improvements to engine bearings, the lubrication system and the clutch. The engine, with a single Linkert carburettor, was coupled to a three-speed gearbox via a foot-operated multi-disc clutch and open chain drive to the rear wheel. Lower ratio gears were used in the transmission to better suit the machine to slow-speed operation. Like the WL, the machine rode on 18in wheels fitted with 4.00 section Firestone road tyres. Wide-section mudguards without side skirts were fitted and these provided increased clearance to prevent a build-up of mud.

Plenty of torque was available from the engine to push the machine through the rough stuff, but this was not an off-road motorcycle. Unfortunately, poor ground clearance – little more than 4in (10cm) – tended to militate against off-road riding conditions. On the road, despite somewhat poor acceleration, the WLA was capable of approximately 65mph (105kph) which was very good considering the machine weighed nearly 600lb (272kg). It also proved to be extremely reliable.

Right: Photographed at Fort Jackson, South Carolina, in February 1943, these two WLA riders are on practice manoeuvres. Note the British-type blackout mask on the headlamp of each machine. (NA)

Below: Bouncing uncomfortably over rough terrain, Charles H. Parker of the US 1st Reconnaissance Division uses his WLA for a scouting trip in Sicily in July 1943. (NA)

Left: The location is Fort Jackson, South Carolina and Private First Class Harold Dearborn shows off his motorcycling skills having never ridden a machine before joining the army. (NA)

Right: The Indian 340, seen here with its distinctive sidecar, was the nearest rival to the sidecar-equipped Model U. Large numbers of the former were supplied to the UK. (FC)

Below: The US Army military-pattern sidecar changed little since it was introduced into service in the early 1900s. The same body was fitted to Canadian Army WLCs. (DC/BVMM)

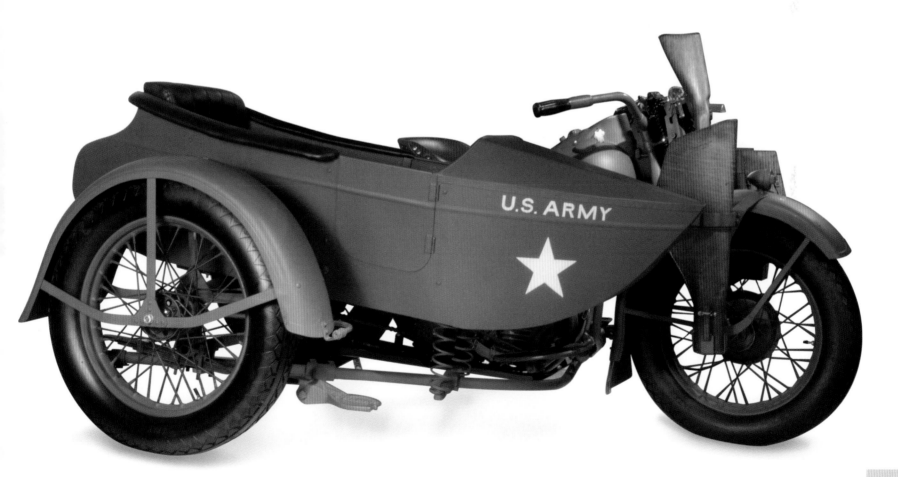

The front forks on the prototypes were parallelogram 'I' section beam girder design as used on the Model RL, with twin coil-springs for suspension and an adjustable steering damper. The rear end was typically 'solid', relying on a softly sprung generous-sized leather saddle to cushion the rider from road shocks. Additional fittings for the military variant included a lower chain guard, heavy engine skid-protection plate and side crash bars.

It was more-or-less in this form that the WLA went into production in March 1940, although the front forks were re-designed using the tubular style of the WL, and were extended by 2.75in (7cm) when compared to the standard, to provide increased ground clearance. Some early examples were fitted with pillion seats – 'buddy seats' in US parlance. The WLA was used only as a solo machine by the US Army, but the Model WLC (Canada), was also occasionally fitted with a pillion seat, and sometimes found mounted with a Goulding single-seat sidecar, in which form it may have been described as Model WLS.

Above: Photographed in November 1943, these are motorcycle messengers of Base Section 3 Message Center, Brisbane, Queensland, Australia. The machines are WLAs but there is a mixture of dates and at least one has a civilian-style front mudguard suggesting an earlier model. (NA)

Right: May 1945: traffic control officers of the US Military Police used motorcycles to direct motor convoy movements and traffic in port areas. (NA)

Left and below: This curious machine with twinned rear wheel dates from when members of the Army Desert Training Center at Indio, California modified a WLA by mounting a pair of close-coupled rear wheels, designed to improve traction. (FC)

Right: During World War Two, the US Army was strictly segregated along race lines. This photograph, taken in April 1942, shows an MP on an early WLA. (NA)

No production figures are available for 1940. For 1941, the WLA was fitted with a large oil-bath air cleaner, as well as being equiped with a rear rack and leather pannier bags; it also carried a leather machine-gun scabbard on the right-hand front fork, and an ammunition box fitted high on

Above: Did they ever really do this? Mechanised troops of the US Army, 100th Cavalry Regiment demonstrate an unusual method of throwing down the motorcycle and using it as cover and gun support during manoeuvres. Note the engine skid plate. (NA)

Left: The US Army 107th Cavalry Regiment being trained for conversion from horse mounts to motorcycles. The date is May 1942 and the column includes Harley-Davidson WLAs and Willys Jeeps. (NA)

the left-hand fork. For winter weather, metal leg shields were also available, together with a windshield fitted with a leatherette-fabric apron. The glossy green finish of the original prototypes was long gone and, visually, there was not a hint of chrome or brightwork anywhere and, aside from the black-painted cylinders and a dull aluminium crankcase, the machine was painted olive drab, including wheel rims and spokes.

The WLA was now also joined by the WLC, the latter intended for the Canadian Army and available in what were described as 'domestic' and 'export' models, both incorporating a number of detailed changes when compared

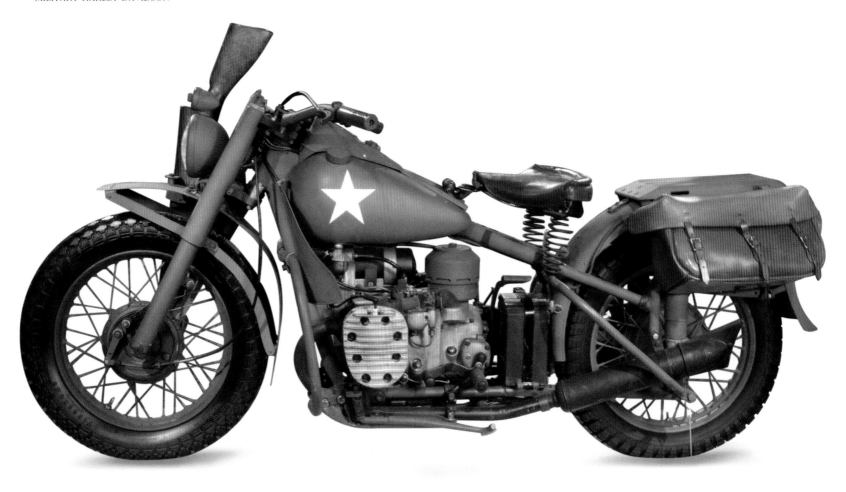

to the WLA. These included British-style right-hand clutch-and-throttle configuration, with the ignition-timing lever also on the right. There were a number of differences in the lighting arrangements, which tended to reflect British military practice; there was also a different instrument nacelle, slightly-smaller mudguards, and an ammunition/spare parts box carried on the front mudguard. The WLC was not fitted with the rifle scabbard or ammunition box as on the US Army machines.

Although the US Army generally preferred not to meddle with with proven designs, particularly once they had been 'standardised', an interesting 3x2 version of the WLA was produced in 1941 in an attempt to improve the traction of motorcycles in desert conditions. A standard production WLA (registration number USA 64693 from contract QM-8356) was fitted with twin 18in rear wheels on a

common axle, the wheels set some 6in (32mm) apart by the use of a pair of offset rear forks. There was no differential, which must have made cornering somewhat tricky, and the drive chain was connected to a sprocket fitted to the inner face of the left-hand wheel. The prototype, which may have been constructed by Army personnel, was tested at the US Army Desert Training Center, Indio, California in July 1942, but there was no series production.

Above: Designed on the lines of captured BMW and Zündapp used by the *Wehrmacht*, the Harley-Davidson Model XA had a horizontally-opposed engine and shaft drive. Intended for the deserts of North Africa, only a relatively small number were produced. (DC/BVMM)

Right: Oran, North Africa, 1942. A WLA with twin rear lights; on Indian machines the lights were mounted one above the other. (NA)

Left: Mounted on a late model WLA, motorcycle messenger Private Harold Peters of the US Army 6th Armored Division, struggles along a muddy track in Nancy, France.(NA)

Production for the year 1941 amounted to 2,282 examples of the WLA and 149 of the WLC. Two examples of the WLC were supplied to the British War Office (WD numbers were allocated as C4782631 and C4782632) for trials, but the British Army does not appear to have taken any further deliveries.

Further changes were made in 1942 when the machine finally evolved into its standardised form, with blackout driving lamps (these were not fitted to the 'domestic' Model WLC), radio-frequency suppressed plug connectors, and rectangular air cleaner (from mid–1942); the bicycle-pedal type kick starter was also superseded by a spool-type pedal. On the WLA only, the ammunition box was moved to lower down the forks and the positions of the horn and headlamp were swapped, putting the headlamp lower down – the blackout driving lamp was fitted alongside it. Although the pillion seat was no longer fitted, some examples carried a separate rear seat which necessitated a change to the rear rack, or its complete omission. In the interests of standardisation, the front forks reverted to the normal length, and stayed that way for the remainder of the machine's production life. Production in 1942 totalled 13,051 for the WLA, and 9,820 for the WLC.

There were no significant modifications for 1943, although aficionados will point to a change in the shape of the front mudguard, the deletion of the name 'Harley-Davidson' from the footrest mats, a change to canvas as the material for the windshield apron, and the fact that the ignition switch no longer required a key. The repositioning of the headlamp and horn, which had been made to the WLA the previous year, now appeared on the WLC. Production totalled 24,717 of the WLA, together with 2,647 of the WLC.

Further radio suppression equipment was fitted in 1944, and machines so equipped were indicated by the letter 'S' stencilled onto the instrument panel nacelle. The US government cancelled contracts for 11,331 motorcycles in February 1944, but production for the year still amounted to 11,531 WLAs and 5,356 WLCs. It is worth noting that the detail changes to

the machine described above did not necessarily coincide in production with the roll-over from one year to the next.

In 1944, an experimental sidecar-equipped machine with all-wheel drive (as on *Wehrmacht* machines) was prepared for the Soviet Army; designated Model WSR. Essentially this was a WLA to which had been fitted leg shields and a winter windscreen, together with a single-seat driven-wheel sidecar with cutaway sides and a windshield. The sidecar

Above: A column of WLA on manouevres somewhere in the USA. (USQM)

Right: The motorcycles are WLAs but it hardly matters. In truth, any motorcycle would have kicked up the same amount of dust and necessitated the wearing of the same protective clothing. (PW)

carried a spare wheel on the rear and all of the wheels were interchangeable. The sidecar may possibly have been manufactured by Goulding.

All remaining military motorcycle contracts were cancelled in August 1945, but production for the year totalled 8,317 examples of the WLA, with the WLC already deleted from the catalogue.

Technical specification

Models WLA, WLC.

Engine:
737cc (45cu.in) Harley-Davidson '45'; two cylinders in 45° 'V' formation; bore and stroke, 2.76in x 3.9in (70mm x 98mm); side valves; dry sump; air cooled; power output, 23bhp at 4600rpm; torque, 28 lbf/ft at 3000rpm.

Transmission:
3F, hand gear-change; multi-plate wet clutch; duplex primary chain running in closed casing; exposed roller-chain drive to rear wheel; primary and secondary chains on left-hand side of motor.

Suspension:
parallelogram leading-link steel-tube front forks with twin coil springs, friction damped; solid rear forks. Steel parallelogram leading-link I-beam front forks used on prototypes.

Brakes:
mechanical by rod and cable, front and rear.

Tyre size:
4.00-18, front and rear; optional, 5.50-16 desert tyres available, bead lock used on the rear wheel to prevent tyre creep.

Construction:
cycle type steel-tube frame.

Electrical system:
6V.

Dimensions
Length, 88in (2.24m); *width,* 36.25in (92cm); *height,* (with windshield) 59in (1.45m), (without windshield) 41in (1.04m).
Wheelbase, 57.5in (1.46m).
Ground clearance, 4in (102mm).
Unladen weight, 515lb (234kg).

Performance
Maximum permitted speed, 65mph (105kph).
Range of action, 125 miles (201km).
Average fuel consumption, 41mpg (14.5kpl).

Production machines had at first been identified with the 39-WLA, 40-WLA and 41-WLK following the company's normal practice, but as the war progressed, the serial numbers were not changed in the normal way, and all production between 1942 and 1945 was identified as 42-WLA – some say that this was done so as not to give the enemy any possible hints as to the output of the factory in any given year – certainly, when production of the WLA resumed in 1949, the frame numbering system reverted to normal. Similarly, all Canadian Army machines were identified as either 42-WLC or 43-WLC, regardless of the year of manufacture. Contrary to normal practice, the frames were not stamped with any serial number. The only identifying number appeared on the engine crankcase and, for late-production machines, also on the military data plate.

Modern-day enthusiasts for the 42-WLA have identified seven distinct combinations of modification fitted to production machines between September 1941 and August 1945. These can be identified by registration number.

In all, about 78,000 examples were constructed between 1940 and August 1945 – 60,000 of these went to the US forces, 30,000 reputedly went to the USSR, and the remainder were

Above: Impressive formation of US Army despatch riders practise a sychronised start-up whilst undergoing training. (USQM)

Right: The XA was designed largely by John Nowak, and was said to have been based on a captured BMW R-12 (shown). Like the BMW, the XA featured a horizontally-opposed side-valve engine, with a separate carburettor for each cylinder. The photograph was taken at the 'War & Peace Show' at Beltring, Kent in July 2006. (ST)

supplied to the various Allies, including Australia, India, China and others. Of course, WLCs went to Canada.

There is no evidence that the British Army officially used any significant numbers of WLAs; the type does not appear in the wartime 'key list' of vehicles in service, nor in the 1946 'nomenclature' list although the equivalent Indian motorcycle appears in both. The RAF certainly had access to some of the Canadian WLCs. However, this does not mean that WLAs were not seen on the British roads during World War Two, it just means that they were US Army machines. The average price of a WLA throughout World War Two was $380.

When the military contracts were cancelled, large numbers of WLAs became available on the civilian market on both sides of the Atlantic, sometimes in brand new unissued condition; huge numbers were disposed of after 1945. Many were resprayed and offered for sale in a 'civilian' form. Of those machines which remained in military service, many were rebuilt and supplied to various European armies, including those of France, Belgium and the Netherlands, as part of the post-war Marshall Plan.

For some curious reason, there was some very limited production of the WLA for the US Army, alongside the WL, during the period 1949 to 1952, amounting to 78,000.

Right: Unlike British motorcycles of the period, the Harley-Davidsons retained a hand gear-change, seen here on the left-hand side of the fuel tank. A Canadian Army despatch rider (note badge) consults a route map. (NAC)

Left: Canadian Model WLC with standard factory sidecar fitted on the left-hand side. (NAC)

MODEL XA

The XA is the closest there is to a purpose-built military Harley-Davidson. Inspired by the horizontal twin-cylinder BMW-built motorcycles used by the *Wehrmacht* since 1929, Harley-Davidson built 1,000 or 1,011 Model XAs exclusively

for the US Army under contract QM-9640 between 1941 and 1943. Although the XA was powered by a 737cc (45cu.in) two-cylinder horizontally-opposed engine, with almost exactly the same capacity as the WLA. The XA actually shared very little in design with other models in the company's range.

The Model XA – the designation was supposed to have stood for 'experimental, army' – was intended for use in the desert war which was raging in 1941. The machine was developed from a specification drawn up by the US War Department in 1941 describing a specialised, shaft-driven military motorcycle. Indian, GM-Delco, and Harley-Davidson were all invited to compete for a production contract which could have a run of 25,000 units. The equivalent Indian,

Above: A lone Harley-Davidson WLC among British-built Nortons of the 48th Highlanders during an exercise in England, 19 April 1943. (NAC)

Left: A Canadian Army despatch rider mounted on a WLC is handed a message from a pigeon loft attendant of the Royal Canadian Corps of Signals, England, 10 February 1943. (NAC)

Above: A well-restored Harley-Davidson WLC as delivered to the Canadian Army. (JBn)

Left: Running adjustments to a pair of WLCs; note the map case and satchel on the right-hand machine. The despatch rider is at 2nd Canadian Corps Headquarters during exercise SPARTAN in England, 12 March, 1943. (NAC)

of which 1,000 were also purchased, was the shaft-driven Model 841.

Designed largely by John Nowak, the XA was said to have been based on a captured BMW R-12. Like the BMW, the XA featured a horizontally-opposed side-valve engine, with a separate carburettor for each cylinder. A distributor-less automatic advance ignition system (which sparked both plugs on every upstroke) was fitted. The double-throw crankshaft meant that a flywheel was not required.

In truth, this was not Harley-Davidson's first use of the horizontally-opposed twin, the 584cc (35.64cu.in) Model WF, dating from 1919, had featured just such an engine, albeit with the cylinders aligned along the main axis of the frame. The US Army had trialled three of these machines in 1919 but made no further purchases. For the XA, the engine was turned so that the cylinders were placed across the frame, into the air flow, with heat shields fitted to protect the rider's

133

Left and below: Some of these motorcycles, in US Army maintenance training facility, look decidedly well used. Note the sidecar chassis on the right in the lower photograph. (USQM)

Right: With a blackout light, white-painted mudguard ends and masked-out headlamp, this MP is obviously expecting to do some serious night-time driving. The machine is a WLA. (DD)

US QUARTERMASTER CORPS AND ORDNANCE DEPARTMENT CONTRACTS FOR THE WLA/WLC

Date	Contract	Quantity	US Army registration numbers
			(all US Army motorcycle registration numbers were prefixed '6')
1940	QM-7238	2	USA 61995-61996
	QM-7518	410	USA 63316-63725
	QM-7737	11	USA 63746-63756
1941	QM-8356	651	USA 64291-64939, USA 65443-65444
	QM-9098	1,800	USA 65448-66647, USA 67848-68447
	QM-10530	4,800	USA 610000-614687, USA 69888-69999
1942	QM-11782*	31,913	USA 616923-637235, USA 671621-683220
1943	2849 (Ordnance Dept)	9,171	USA 686726-694000, USA 694006-695001
1944	11-022-381 (Ordnance Dept)	13,811	USA 6110920-6124730
1945	n/a	8,201	USA 6128521-6133520, USA 6138558-6141758**
1949	n/a	436	n/a
1950	n/a	15	n/a
1951	n/a	1	n/a
1952	n/a	2	n/a

Total supplied, 1940 to 1952, according to Harley-Davidson production records: 78,353

* These vehicles also listed under Ordnance Department contract 2498.

** These registration numbers were assigned to 1945 production but may not actually have been issued.

boots from the hot cylinder heads. It was believed that the 180° horizontally-opposed design would make it easier to keep engine temperature down in the heat of the North African desert. Reportedly, the engine oil temperature ran 100°F (38°C) cooler than a standard air-cooled V-twin such as the WLA. Combined with the inherently-smoother operation of the engine, this gave an anticipated life of 10,000 to 15,000 miles (16,093 to 24,139km).

Again, following the lead of the German machine, the XA was shaft-driven. The *Wehrmacht* had already discovered that the dust and grit of the desert quickly damaged a conventional roller-chain drive and realised that shaft drive was the only way to achieve reliability. A four-speed constant-mesh gearbox, similar to that used on the WLA, drove the rear wheel through a flexible rubber coupling, then via an exposed universal-jointed propeller shaft to a crown wheel and pinion gear set.

Other features intended to cope with the arduous desert conditions included increased ground clearance with the use of a large skid plate fitted under the engine and high-clearance mudguards, particularly at the rear. An oil bath-type air filter was fitted to the engine. In a break with Harley-Davidson tradition, the clutch was hand operated with a lever on the right-hand side of the handlebars. The gearshift was foot operated in European style, but with an auxiliary hand control also fitted on the handlebars. The front end featured a lengthened, friction-damped version of the WLA fork assembly. Telescopic coil-spring suspension dampers were fitted at the rear. A handful of machines constructed in 1943 were fitted with a lengthened frame in which the engine was positioned a little further back, and these were the first

Harley-Davidson motorcycles to be fitted with telescopic front forks.

The wheels were of the standard 18in diameter used on the WLA fitted with both 4.00 and 5.00 rims. Most machines were fitted with spoked wheels, but of the 1,000 Model XA motorcycles built in 1941, between 50 and 100 were delivered with 15in x 6in solid disc wheels. It was thought that this type of wheel would be more durable in sand and stone desert conditions.

A strong rack-type carrier was fitted on the rear, designed to carry a 40lb (18kg) radio receiver, together with saddlebags, ammunition box and other stowed items.

Although the machine was described as the '42-XA' mass production, such as it was, took place only in 1941. The military registration numbers ran from USA 614903 to 615902. Each of the machines built was said to have cost $870, compared to an average price of $380 for the WLA. None were sent into combat, but were shipped to Camp Holabird, Maryland and Fort Knox, Kentucky, also Fort Carson, Colorado for evaluation and training purposes.

As the trials progressed, problems came to light with the engine lubrication system and the valve gear. These problems could almost certainly have been solved, but the Ordnance Department was undecided on the project. There was talk of an order for a further 25,000 XAs in place of the same number of WLAs. By the time the US government was ready to award the contract, the war in North Africa was virtually at an end. The Jeep had been successfully used for the roles for which the XA had been considered.

The GM-Delco motorcycle never even reached the pre-production stage. Neither the Harley-Davidson XA nor the Indian 841 entered series production. The XA project was effectively terminated in 1943.

At least one example designated Model XAS was experimentally fitted with a driven-wheel sidecar. Drive to the sidecar wheel was by means of a cross-shaft driven by a crownwheel and pinion. Several modifications were made to the basic production XA, including the use of Firestone 5.50-16 tractor-type tyres and a high-level exhaust system. A passenger seat and grab bars were fitted to the motorcycle. The single-seat sidecar, which was not the standard civilian

Technical specification

Model XA.

Classification:
not classified.

Engine:
739cc (45.10cu.in) Harley-Davidson XA;
two cylinders, horizontally-opposed;
bore and stroke, 3.1in x 3.1in (78mm
x 78mm); overhead valves; dry sump;
air cooled; power output, 23bhp at
4,600rpm.

Transmission:
4 gears; foot-pedal and hand gear-
change; single-plate dry clutch;
rubber-damped exposed shaft drive to
rear wheel.

Suspension:
parallelogram leading-link steel-tube
front forks with twin-coil spring;
friction damped; experimental
telescopic front forks on 1943 models;
sprung telescopic rear suspension.

Brakes:
mechanically operated drum brakes;
front and rear.

Tyre size:
4.00-18 or 5.00-18 spoked, or 6.00-15
solid disc; same size front and rear.

Construction:
duplex steel-tube frame.

Electrical system:
6V battery.

Dimensions
Length, 90in (2.3m); *width*, 36in (91cm);
height, (with windscreen) 60in (1.5m),
(without windscreen) 40.25in (102cm).
Wheelbase, 59.5in (1.5m).
Ground clearance, 6.1in (155mm).
Unladen weight, 525lb (238kg).

Performance
Maximum allowable speed, 60mph
(97kph).
Range of action, 150 miles (241km).
Average fuel consumption, 38mpg
(13.5kpl).

Above, both: The shaft-drive XA was an attempt to emulate the heavy motorcycles which the *Afrika Korps* had used so effectively in North Africa. The 739cc (45.10cu.in) horizontally-opposed side-valve engine was arranged across the frame in an attempt to improve cooling to the cylinders. (Left: DC/BVMM. Above: PW)

type, had a cut-away side (in the style of a Jeep) for ease of entry and exit. A pressed steel Jeep-style mudguard was fitted as was an enclosed locker at the rear. The spare wheel was mounted on the front of the sidecar.

Harley-Davidson also experimented with the XA engine in a civilian three-wheeled model which they considered selling after the war. The engine was supplied to Willys to power an experimental lightweight Jeep.

Also it was supplied to manufacturers of military-type stationery generators. It is rumoured that two of these engines were coupled to provide motive power for a light tank. Unfortunately no details have been found.

The Model XA was never offered to the civilian market, nor was any of the technology developed incorporated into Harley-Davidson's post-war products. The company's 1942 technical manual explicitly states 'the XA model motorcycle is a special motorcycle built for the Army according to Army specifications no spare parts or service tools are available it will be of no avail to attempt to secure parts or tools by ordering direct from the factory according to the part and tool numbers shown in this manual'. Of course, many examples, often with very low mileage, subsequently became available through military surplus outlets after 1945. A number survive to this day and are much sought after by military enthusiasts.

Restoration

In 1944, a military surplus Harley-Davidson WLA cost around $450, little more than £100. Sixty years later, such machines, now highly sought after and much prized, regularly change hands at more than £10,000. All vintage Harley-Davidsons have acquired iconic status, but the military machines have a following all their own. Hundreds survive across the world and the mortal remains of others which once might have been considered beyond salvation are being dragged from barns and scrapyards to be meticulously restored.

CHAPTER 5 RESTORATION

With the increases in disposable income which followed the steady improvements in standards of living across the Western world in the decades following the end of the war, many have come to regard the preservation of antique machinery as a legitimate hobby. Thousands of pounds and dollars are lavished on vehicles which are used only occasionally and which, in truth, are often totally unsuited to modern traffic conditions.

With the war over, Harley-Davidson went straight back to the business of building motorcycles for the civilian market. It was hard work at first, perhaps not helped by the fact that, from 1944 onwards, thousands of surplus Harley-Davidsons, some almost new, had been put up for sale by US government at $450 each. Most were WLAs since these had been built in the greatest numbers, but there were also low-mileage XAs at just $500, a machine for which most military motorcycle enthusiasts today would be prepared to mortgage everything.

There was also some following for these machines in the UK with a few dealers specialising in Harley-Davidsons. One such dealer was Pride & Clark in South London. However, most British riders tended to prefer British motorcycles which were also widely available on the surplus market and were better suited to home road conditions.

Understandably, there was no interest in restoring old military machinery back in 1945 and most surplus vehicles, were either 'civilianised', having the military equipment removed and being sprayed with a more colourful finish, or were simply run as they were with parts replaced as and when necessary. Surplus parts were equally plentiful and,

anyway, the old 737cc (45cu.in) side-valve V-twin remained in production for many years after the war.

In the US, some of these World War Two machines were customised to make them faster or to better express the rider's personality. 'Bobbing' became popular, where the big front tyre was replaced by one with a very narrow 3in (76mm) section, the rear mudguard was shortened, and a small seat was mounted directly onto the frame. This was later called the 'easy rider' or 'chopper' look. Parts were removed to reduce weight and street racing became almost as popular as the legitimate track-based sport.

This was the beginning of the 'rebel' motorcycle scene which led to such hysteria following the disturbance at the town of Hollister, California on 4 July 1947 (the event is celebrated with an annual motorcycle rally, now in its 60th year), and eventually gave birth to the Hells Angels Motorcycle Club. These events were dramatised in the subsequent film *The Wild One* starring Lee Marvin and Marlon Brando. Many motorcycles were driven to destruction or wrecked in accidents and no one thought much about the military origins of the machines.

Above: A superbly restored Harley-Davidson WLA, one of many, displayed at the Barber Vintage Motorcyle Museum, Birmingham, Alabama. (DC/BVMM)

Previous pages: A well restored and correctly equipped Harley-Davidson WLA. Note the bracket which allowed the fitting of leg guards. (PR)

Gradually the stocks of surplus motorcycles, and the parts required to keep them running, began to disappear.

But, around the same time that the war surplus machines started to disappear, a handful of British and US vehicle enthusiasts realised that these military motorcycles were worth saving. Dwindling stocks of original parts were purchased and hoarded, machines were dragged from scrapyards and painstakingly restored, and those which had been heavily modified for a civilian life were returned to original form. Peter Gray, founder of the Military Vehicle Conservation Group (now the Military Vehicle Trust), was one of the first to ride a fully-restored military Harley-Davidson.

Soon the enthusiasts started coming together in clubs. In the UK, the Military Vehicle Conservation Group (later the Military Vehicle Trust) was founded in 1968; the US Military Vehicle Preservation Association dates back to 1976. Similar organisations now exist in France, Canada, Belgium, the Netherlands, Italy and Ireland. Enthusiasts started to display their vehicles to the public, initially at steam shows and old

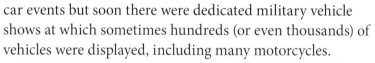

car events but soon there were dedicated military vehicle shows at which sometimes hundreds (or even thousands) of vehicles were displayed, including many motorcycles.

Whilst those early restorations tended to be 'generic', gradually the more dedicated enthusiasts started to painstakingly research the history of the motorcycles and to pin down the many minor changes that had been made during production. Historians of the 42-WLA identified and documented seven distinct combinations of modification which were incorporated between September 1941 and August 1945. These can be identified by frame or registration number, and restorers are prepared to go to great lengths to ensure that a motorcycle is absolutely 'right' for its date of manufacture.

There are several dealers who now specialise in buying and selling these machines and in supplying parts. Although reproduction parts are available, many original items have survived and almost any old motorcycle can be brought back to life. A copy of the long out-of-print 'bible' on Harley-Davidson restoration: *How to Restore your Military Harley-Davidson* by Bruce Palmer can cost upwards of $200 when one is available for sale, which is not often.

The military Harley-Davidson has acquired a considerable following and a well-restored example can sell for a five-figure sum; one particularly well-restored WLA was recently offered in the UK at £12,000. The owner of an original XA could practically name his own price since only a handful

Far left: With its unique horizontally-opposed engine, the XA was more akin to a German-built BMW than to the traditional Harley-Davidson product line; note the steel leg shields and the inevitable leather rifle scabbard. (DC/BVMM)

Left (both): Detail of the Model XA engine. (DC/BVMM)

Right: Since more than 78,000 were constructed, it should be little surprise that most restored bikes are of the Model WLA. (JBn)

Following pages: With the ammunition box at the front, rifle scabbard, saddlebags and blackout lights, this WLA looks much as it must have done when it entered military service back in 1944. (PR)

of these machines survive. There is now the beginning of an enthusiast base for the comparatively recent Harley-Davidson (Armstrong) MT350 and MT500 models.

Today, interest in old military vehicles is a huge worldwide phenomenon and interest in military Harley-Davidsons is a vital component of that movement.

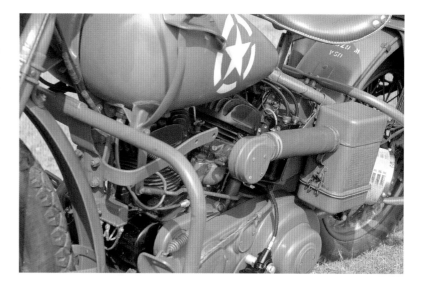

Left: Enthusiasts continue to argue over the correct shade of colour for a World War Two bike and it is almost impossible to get any agreement. Some argue for a khaki brown; others are equally insistent that it was green. (PR)

Right: The other colour in which some enthusiasts argue that the military Harley-Davidsons were painted. (PR)

Below left: On late-model WLAs the bicycle pedal starter was replaced by a simple spool pedal. This view also shows the rear brake pedal protruding through the footboard. This machine lacks the skidplate under the engine and transmission. (PR)

Below: Thank goodness for enthusiasts! A well restored Dodge WC 54 weapons carrier and a splendid Harley-Davidson WLA. (PR)

Left: Military vehicle enthusiats discuss the route of the parade during the 6oth anniversary of the D-Day landings, 6 June 2004. (JBn)

Right: The early air cleaner was cylindrical in design. (JBn)

Below: Dating from 1937, the big Model U was popular with the US Navy. This machine was used in Guam and is displayed at the Barber Vintage Motorcycle Museum, Birmingham, Alabama. (DC/BVMM)

Left: The .45 calibre M1A1 Thompson sub-machine gun (SMG), sometimes nicknamed 'The Gangster Gun', or in British service 'The Tommy Gun', fitted nicely into the leather scabbard. (JSS)

Below left: A nicely-restored WLA accessorised with a few period items. The chain securing the machine gun to the motorcycle is a non-standard item, fitted purely for security by the owner. (JBn)

Below and right: Early speedometers were coloured up to 1942 when the face was changed to olive drab and the lettering beige. The switch below the speedo face is for the ignition. Note how the oil tank for the dry sump engine forms part of the fuel tank. (JBn)

Above: This WLA has the headlamp in the original position above the horn. (JBn)

Right: Three gear-shifter gates were used during the life of the WLA. Originally, the civilian gate was used but in 1942 it was simplified; on post-war WLAs the gear pattern was reversed (3, 2, N, 1 rather than 1, N, 2, 3) and the gate was reshaped again. The photograph shows the earliest design. (JBn)

Above left: The rear mudguard carried a pair of side-by-side rear lights and the US Army registration number. (JBn)

Top right: They're only original once and this speedo has a lovely original patina. (JBn)

Bottom right: Ammunition carrier on the front forks. (JBn)

Following spread: Three WLAs and a Dodge weapons carrier: olive-drab heaven! The far machine is fitted with brackets for leg shields. (PR)

Finale

The post-war years were something of a roller coaster for Harley-Davidson. Although military sales came to an abrupt end in 1945, the company introduced some of its best-known models during the fifties and even took a segment of the small bike market. On the corporate front there were two changes of ownership and near-bankruptcy but the company's fortunes seem to have finally been turned around, albeit the military motorcycle is almost a thing of the past.

CHAPTER 6 FINALE

Harley-Davidson had manufctured something like 88,000 military motorcycles during the war years but the machines never found the widespread use that had been envisaged by the military and large numbers had already been disposed of by the spring and summer of 1944. When the war in Europe ended in May 1945, thousands of surplus military vehicles were put up for sale in the USA and amongst these were 15,000 WLAs, offered at a government-controlled price of $450.

Civilian production, which had come to an end on 9 February 1942, resumed almost as soon as fighting in the deserts of North Africa was over, but Harley-Davidson was not able to offer anything more than what were basically the pre-war models. Even then, material shortages meant that there was a decided lack of chrome and, for a few months, the machines were distinctly drab looking. Many enthusiasts still feel that it was a great pity that the shaft-drive Model XA was not offered to the civilian market after the war but there were presumably good reasons.

However, thanks to 'Uncle Sam', Harley-Davidson had been able to make considerable investments during the war years, investing some $1,000,000 in plant and tooling. But, of course, there had been no direct development in civilian motorcycles and there were no new models on the stocks. When the first all-new post-war model was released in 1948 it was greeted with great excitement by the motorcycling public and, whilst it might have been big news, for what were not necessarily the right reasons, the new Model S, must have been distinctly under-whelming to those used to the big, V-twin engined Harley-Davidsons of the previous 40 years.

The Model S was a diminutive single-cylinder two-stroke machine with 'rubber band' suspension on the front forks and a distinctly cycle-like steel frame. It was derived from the German-designed DKW RT125 which had been used widely during the war by *Wehrmacht troops*. The Model S did go on to sell a creditable number of units, perhaps helping to expand the leisure biking market outside of its pre-war demographics but, beyond a head-to-head test with the Indian Model 144, the model S was never used by the US military in anger.

Right: The World War Two WLA remained in service with the US Army into the 1950s, the Army continuing to buy small numbers of the machine, virtually unchanged, between 1949 and 1952. Most were used for Military Police duties as here on New Caledonia, an island in the southwest Pacific ocean. (NA)

Previous pages: Members of 45 Commado Motor Transport on exercise in Devon, southwest England. The despatch rider is mounted on a Rotax-engined Harley-Davidson MT350E. (MoD)

Above: The last use of the 737cc (45cu.in) V-twin engine was in the 'Servi-Car' which remained in production until 1973, but the big side-valve 'traditional' Harley-Davidson remained a popular choice for law enforcement units, seen here with outriders at Franklin D. Roosevelt's funeral on 1 January 1945. (NA)

Far right: Jeep and motorcycle outriders at a parade in honour of Fleet Admiral Chester W. Nimitz, travel along Pennsylvania Avenue, New York City on 5 October 1945. (NA)

In the same year, and perhaps of more interest to the traditional Harley-Davidson fan, the company also launched the so-called 'Panhead' engine by fitting both the 999cc (61cu.in) and 1,311cc (74cu.in) power units with hydraulic valve lifters and aluminium cylinder heads. It was the shape of the new chrome-plated rocker cover that gave the engine its nickname but the new engine was more powerful than the units it replaced and remained standard until 1966.

Development of the civilian machines picked up pace during the 1950s and features such as hydraulic front forks, over-head valve engines and electric starters became standard items. But there were to be no more purpose-designed military machines by Harley-Davidson. Granted, the US Army continued to buy wartime-specification WLAs in small numbers through to 1952, but these were by no means new models, the most significant change being the reversal of the gear-shift pattern.

This was generally a period in which military interest in the big Harley-Davidson style of motorcycle dropped to almost zero. For the 1950s and 1960s, the British were buying lighter home-designed products, as were the French and Germans. The Dutch and Belgian Armies had purchased a few, essentially civilian, 'Electra-Glides' for convoy escort and

Military Police duties, but they were on their own. By 1963, the US Army placed its last contract with the company when some 400 militarised XL 'Sportsters' were purchased.

By the end of the 1960s the big military Harley-Davidson was effectively a thing of the past.

Motorcycles were reconsidered for various roles during the fuel-starved 1970s but in practice these were more likely to be light machines than big-engined Harley-Davidsons.

From the company's point of view, there was a small revival when in 1987 Harley-Davidson purchased the British company Armstrong, which had been supplying the Rotax-engined MT500 trailbike to the British Army, and others, since 1985. At the time, Harley-Davidson, which was also using Rotax engines on other machines, was keen to supply motorcycles to NATO, but the company had also

Left: South African Military Police on what are almost certainly World War Two-vinatge Model WLAs. (SANMMH)

Right: Well turned-out Military Police with WLAs of the US Air Force. (PW)

Below: Early sidecar big-twins, Model US, for transportation attached to Camp Bedilion Acorn Training Detachment, Port Hueneme, California, Note the early cylindrical air cleaners and big windscreens. (NA)

heard a rumour that the US Army was planning to purchase 6,000 motorcycles, which, naturally, they hoped would be their machines. This would have been the most significant purchase of military motorcycles since the end of World War Two but, as it happens, no machines were procured. When the US Army did re-enter the motorcycle market, the machines purchased were of Japanese manufacture.

Harley-Davidson continued to manufacture the MT500 and the subsequent, smaller-engined MT350E, supplying machines to Britain, Jordan and Canada. It is rumoured that a small number of MT500s were used by USAF 'combat control teams'. A total of 4,470 units were built over a 20-year production period, in the UK and in the US. Neither machine was made available through Harley-Davidson dealers. So, the MT was in every sense a strictly-military machine, as had been the XA back in 1941, but it was also notable for being the end of the line as far as the military Harley-Davidson was concerned.

In recent years both the US and British Armies have revived their interest in motorcycles for messenger duties but the mount of the future appears to be a diesel-powered version of the Kawasaki KLR 650.

Left: The distinctive military WLA probably saw a good 20 years of service, both with the US Army and with other services who received war-surplus machines. Thousands also ended up in civilian hands where, often stripped of their utilitarian military fittings, they provided cheap, reliable transportation. (PW)

Right: US Army MPs under training (in the 1950s) manhandle a WLA out of a sandpit. (NA)

Below: US Army GIs practise cross-country riding before seeing active service as despatch riders in Korea during the 1950s. (NA)

Both pages: The Australian Army used Harley-Davidson WLAs during the Korean War (1950 to 1953) for despatch rider duties. (NAA)

MODEL S

Although hardly a 'real' military motorcycle, there are two reasons why the Model S – also known as the 125 – deserves a place in this book. First, the machine had originated in Germany and was used in both civilian and military service the design being acquired by Harley-Davidson as a result of the military reparations in 1945. Secondly, the machine was tested by the US Army as a possible replacement for Indian's lightweight machines being used by airborne forces.

The Model S first appeared in 1948; the design of the machine was unashamedly copied from the DKW company. Harley-Davidson had acquired the German patents as part of war reparations. The equivalent DKW model was the RT125 which had been introduced in 1939 was quickly adopted by the *Wehrmacht* for messenger and despatch duties. The RT125 was widely used by civilians and remained in production throughout the war, with thousands being produced. The design was also 'adopted' by the East German company MZ and by BSA in Britain, where it appeared, also in 1948, as the Bantam, a motorcycle much loved by British Post Office messengers. The machine was also copied and manufactured by Yamaha in Japan.

The Model S with a 123cc (7.52cu.in) two-stoke side-valve engine and integral three-speed transmission was hardly a classic Harley-Davidson machine – in fact, it was the company's first two-stroke! The engine capacity was increased to 165cc (10.1cu.in) in 1953 for the Model ST by enlarging the bore to 2.4in (60mm). For those who felt the machine was too powerful, the Model STU was offered fitted with restricted carburettor air intake, which limited the top speed. Where later examples of the DKW were fitted with parallelogram-type front forks fitted with a single helical spring damper, Harley-Davidson eschewed such sophistication. The company preferred DKW's earlier type and using 'rubber-band' suspension on the front girder-type forks. No dampers were fitted to the rear forks. Telescopic-type front forks were introduced in 1951, on the 'Tele-Glide' version.

The machine was fitted with proper lighting, with a generator and battery. It is worth noting that at just $325 when introduced, the Model S was priced at approximately half that of a mainstream Harley-Davidson. A total of 10,117

Right: The first Model S was almost an exact copy of the DKW125RT. DKW stands for *DampfkraftWagen* (steam-powered vehicle); a light car produced in 1916. DKW has also stood for *Das Knaben Wunsch* - a boys dream and *Das Kleine Wunder* - a little marvel. (DK)

buyers in the first year, meant that the diminutive 'S' was easily the company's most successful 1948 model.

The Model S was typically European, a single-seater lightweight motorcycle that was cheap to buy and operate, also which could provide basic transportation for all. Harley-Davidson chose to target the younger buyer market, where clearly the machine found some favour. A total of 50,000 units were sold during a 12-year production run perhaps this was down to Harley-Davidson's snappy advertising slogan: 'it's the slickest thing on wheels'!

The US Army took delivery of one or more of these machines in 1948 for possible airborne use – the Indian Model 144 having been used in this role during Word War Two. At that time, Harley-Davidson had no equivalent machine but the appearance of the Model S changed this, and was used in 'head to head' trials with the post-war Indian Model 148 at Aberdeen Proving Ground, Maryland. It appears that the Model S was not a success and was not purchased. The US Army's airborne forces continued to use the Indian machine, subsequently replacing the 148 with the company's later Model 149M.

MODEL K

In appearance, the new Model K was more of a modern motorcycle. Low and compact, with the chrome, telescopic-type front forks disappearing into the integral nacelle which housed the speedometer and headlamp. The machine was a great improvement over the old Model W and was intended to meet the challenge of imported British 500cc and 650cc machines head-on. Sadly, the Model K was too slow, suffered from ponderous handling and unreliability, the new transmission causing most problems. Giving a weight advantage to the imports of around 100lb (45.4kg), the model proved to be something of an anachronism and, with the out-dated side-valve engine, was probably obsolete even before the machine was introduced. The range was advertised

under the slogan, 'America's most sensational motorcycle', and was launched with a single standard model. The range was supplemented by the smaller-framed, stripped-down Models KR and KRTT – the latter sold as a 'Tourist Trophy' machine, but both were intended for racing. The launch price for the street machine was $865, and sales for the first year stood at a lowly 1,970 examples, including 17 examples of the racing KR and KRTT.

The Model K was strictly a solo machine with no matching sidecar being available.

The range was extended in 1953 by the addition of the Model KK, which offered improved performance by using the cams, ports and crankshaft of the KR, but without becoming a pure racing machine. Other changes for the year were minimal, but included a faster-acting throttle and an optional

pillion or 'buddy seat'. The price increased only by $10 to $875, but sales remained disappointing at 1,723. The decision was taken to drop the model from the range.

After just two years in production, during which sales had not reached company expectations, the Model K was replaced by the larger-engined KH. The increase in engine size was achieved by lengthening the stroke to 4.6in (116mm), to allow a capacity of 901cc (55cu.in); although, in truth what was probably needed was a shorter stroke and a larger bore. (British motorcycles, against which the Model KH was competing, offered faster acceleration as well as a higher top speed). The engine's inlet valves were also enlarged and the inlet and exhaust ports were reshaped. Together, these changes gave a useful 12% increase in power output, which necessitated some redesigning of the transmission and

173

Technical specification

Model S.

Engine:
123cc (7.5cu.in) Harley-Davidson '125'; single cylinder; bore and stroke, (2.1in x 2.3in (52mm x 58mm); two stroke; air cooled; power output, 4.3bhp at 4,000rpm.

Transmission:
3 F; foot-pedal gear-change; gearbox unit-constructed with engine; multi-plate wet clutch; exposed roller-chain drive to rear wheel on right-hand side of the engine.

Suspension:
girder front forks with band-type rubber suspension and recoil spring; telescopic forks adopted in 1951; rigid rear fork.

Brakes:
drum brakes, front and rear; mechanically-operated by rod and cable.

Tyre size:
3.25-19; same size front and rear.

Construction:
cycle type steel-tube frame.

Electrical system:
6V battery.

Dimensions
Length, 76in (1.93m); *width*, 26in (66cm); *height*, 35in (89cm).
Wheelbase, 50in (1.27m).
Ground clearance, 5.75in (146mm).
Unladen weight, 175lb (79.4kg).

Performance
Maximum allowable speed, 45mph to 50mph (72kph to 80kph).
Range of action, 165 miles (265.5km).
Average fuel consumption, 95mpg (34kpl).

Left: Although it never saw military service, the little Model S was joined by the ST in 1963 at 165cc (10.2cu.in). The ST offered an additional 40cc (2.5cu.in) of capacity and a bit of extra power. With big saddlebags and fringed saddle, this little chap is masquerading as a 'real' Harley. (DK)

Above: The British-built version of the DKW125RT was the BSA 125cc Bantam, a motorcycle use by 'Telegram Boys' of the GPO (General Post Office). (DC/BVMM)

clutch to improve reliability. The frame and brakes were also redesigned to improve the handling – and stopping – of what was a much more powerful machine. Wheel diameter was reduced to 18in. The price had increased to $925, with sales for the year at 1,579.

Despite the use of a larger engine in the Model KH, the 737cc (45cu.in) engine did not disappear completely for another decade. By using this engine, the Models KR and KRTT remained competitive against larger overhead-valve engined machines under the racing rules of the American Motorcycle Association (AMA). The KR and KRTT continued in production until 1966 and became established as the most successful racing Harley-Davidson ever produced.

Three new models joined the range in 1955: the KHK 'street racer' which featured a special speed kit, racing cams, and polished cylinder heads; the KHRM scrambler; and the KHRTT 'Tourist Trophy' model. Changes for the year included the adoption of a new 1.5in (4cm) Linkert carburettor and better lubrication to the transmission. Steering geometry and front forks were redesigned whilst

the wheels had better hubs and stronger spokes. Although the price for the Model KH remained at $925, this was not enough to revive sales, which amounted to just 616 units for the year. Sales of the racing models remained strong.

The year 1956 saw the end of production for what had proved a very disappointing model. Some further revisions were made to the frame design, which allowed a lower saddle height. Shock absorbers were changed along with a number of other detailed modifications. Sales continued to decline, falling to 539 units for the year, albeit at a price of $935.

Total production of all K series 'street' models – excluding the various racers and pseudo-racers – stood at just 6,357 over a five-year period.

Above: New for 1952 was the 737cc (45cu.in) side-valve Model K, designed to replace the venerable W series. It was not especially successful, but a militarised variant, designated KA, was purchased by the US Army in considerable numbers for Military Police duties. Changes in specification when compared to the civilian machines included the use of a rear carrier rack and rigid side panniers. A small number of examples of the Model KH were also supplied to the Royal Netherlands Army in 1956. (DK)

A militarised variant of the Model K, designated KA, was purchased by the US Army in considerable numbers and was used for Military Police duties. Changes in specification when compared to the civilian machines included the use of a rear carrier rack and rigid side panniers. A small number of

Technical specification

Models K, KA, KH.

Engine:
737cc (45cu.in) or 901cc (55cu.in); Harley-Davidson '45' or '55'; two cylinders in 45° 'V' formation; bore and stroke, 2.76in x 3.8in (70mm x 97mm), or 2.76in x 4.6in (70mm x 116mm); side valves; air cooled; dry sump; power output, 29–38bhp at 4,600rpm.

Transmission:
4 F; foot gear-change; multi-plate dry clutch; triplex primary roller-chain running in closed casing; exposed roller-chain drive to rear wheel; primary chain on left-hand side of the engine, secondary chain on right.

Suspension:
coil spring suspension on front forks, swinging arm with coil springs at rear; hydraulic dampers.

Brakes:
mechanically operated drum brakes; front and rear.

Tyre size:
(1952–53) 3.25-19, (1954–56) 3.50-18, same size front and rear.

Construction:
steel-tube duplex frame.

Electrical system:
6V battery.

Dimensions
Length, 90in (2.3m); *width*, 32in (81cm); *height*, n/a.
Wheelbase, 60in (1.5m).
Ground clearance, 4.5in (114mm).
Unladen weight, 450lb (204kg).

Performance
Maximum allowable speed, 85mph (137kph).
Range of action, n/a.
Average fuel consumption, n/a.

Comprehensive performance and dimensional data was not always available for militarised civilian models.

examples of the civilian Model KH were also supplied to the Royal Netherlands Army in 1956.

MODEL XL 'SPORTSTER'

Introduced for the 1957 model year, and dubbed 'Sportster', the all-new Model XL was effectively a replacement for the, less than successful, KH and was a serious attempt by Harley-Davidson to counter the tide of imported motorcycle. The XL was powered by an all-new 883cc (53.9cu.in) V-twin overhead valve engine, with hemispherical combustion chambers using Harley-Davidson's favoured Imperial measurement. The actual displacement was 53.9cu.in but the company always referred to it as 55cu.in. The modest styling and fairly restrained use of chrome on the Sportster, right down to the use of a circular tank badge, gave the machine something of the appearance of a British motorcycle of the period.

The use of the same 3.8in (97mm) stroke as the original Model K, combined with a wider bore 2.99in (76mm), allowed the engine to rev more freely. The four-cam shaft design made valve operation more reliable and easier to adjust. The choice of cast-iron cylinder heads was considered a little eccentric but, nevertheless, with aluminium-alloy pistons and a Linkert carburettor, the engine produced a very respectable 40bhp at 5,500rpm. This made the Model XL capable of close to 100mph (161kph). The four-speed

transmission featured foot gearchange on the right-hand side of the machine with the clutch operated by a handlebar-mounted lever.

The range was launched with a single model, the touring XL, with no provision for fitting a sidecar. Although the new model was well received by the motorcycle press, sales were disappointingly slow, with just 1,983 machines sold in the first year. Perhaps this had something to do with price: at $1,103, the XL was just $100 more than the much larger Model FL. If you wanted a 'real' Harley-Davidson then the FL would have been more to your taste and if you wanted a British motorcycle, then maybe you were not really in the market for a Harley-Davidson at all.

For the following year, the range was expanded to include four new models: the basic XL was joined by the high-compression XLH. Other additions included the competition XLC, the high-compression competition XLCH and the XLRTT, so-named 'Tourist Trophy' racer. None of these three high-performance models was fitted with a battery or lighting equipment. All three were fitted with magneto ignition, a performance exhaust system. The XL was fitted with the then-fashionable 'bobbed' mudguards which gave the machines an almost customised look. The total number of XL and XLH sold amounted to 1,290, a moderately disappointing figure for what was still a new model.

The lack of sales success for the base Model XL meant that from 1959 the machine was no longer available, although the XLC had already been dropped from the list at the end of 1958. For 1959, changes were made to the fork nacelle and the front mudguard design was revised to include a side skirt. The engine in the XLH and XLCH were fitted with a new design of high-lift camshaft. The XLCH was now also available for street use with the addition of 6V lights powered by a battery and generator system. The Model XL was priced at $1,175, the high-compression models attracting a premium of $25 or $110 (XLRTT). Sales for the Model XL stood at just 42, with a further 2,006 examples sold of the XLH and XLCH.

By 1960, the higher-compression Models XLH and XLHC remained in production with the 883cc (53.9cu.in) engine until 1971. Changes made during this time were minimal but the electrical system was upgraded to 12V in 1965, with electric start incorporated from 1967. The kick-start was removed a year later and at the same time the front forks were improved, whilst the frame was redesigned in 1968. The XLCH lost the racing magneto ignition in favour of a standard coil and distributor in 1970. In 1971 a wet clutch was fitted as standard. Prices for 1960 were $1,225 and $1,310, respectively, with total sales of 2,765 units. By 1971, sales had risen to 11,775. The XLRTT was deleted from the catalogue at the end of 1966.

From 1972, the engine bore was increased to 3.2in (81mm) to give a displacement of 1,000cc (61cu.in) and, in this form, the model stayed in the catalogue until 1985, and was then replaced by the 'Evolution'-engined XLH-883 and XL-1100. The XLH-1200 replaced the XLH-1100 in 1988 and the two models survived until 2002, along with other variations of what had now become the mainstay of the Harley-Davidson range including the Model XLCR 'Café Racer'.

The Model XL saw limited military service, with 418 examples of a lightly-militarised Model XLA being purchased by the US Army and Navy for Military Police work in 1963. Fitted with glass-fibre composite panniers and a windshield, these were presumably medium-compression versions of the XLH. The XLA is notable for being the US Army's last use of the large Harley-Davidson.

Right: The Model XL 'Sportster' appeared in 1957 and was a serious attempt by Harley-Davidson to counter the tide of British imports. The machine was powered by an all-new overhead valve V-twin engine of 883cc (53.9cu.in), with hemispherical combustion chambers and, in its XLA form from 1963, was notable for being the US Army's last use of the large Harley-Davidson. (DK)

MODEL FLB 'ELECTRA-GLIDE'

Strictly speaking, the Model FLB was not entirely new, having originally been introduced as the old Model FL back in 1941, and then, with the addition of telescopic front forks, became the 'Hydra-Glide' in 1949 but 1965 was the first year that the machine was called 'Electra-Glide'. The Model FLB was notable for being the first Harley-Davidson to be fitted with an electric starter, denoted by 'B' being appended to the model designation.

The 'Electra-Glide' range was launched with four models: the FLB was a solo machine with a four-speed hand-shift gearbox. The FLFB was similar but was fitted with hand gear-change. The FLHB and FLFHB followed the same pattern, but were fitted with high-compression cylinder heads for improved performance. Bedecked with chrome-plated accessories, sporting flashy two-tone paint finishes, and weighing in at almost 600lb (272kg), the 'Electra-Glide' was the quintessential Harley-Davidson of the era.

There were many changes compared to the model's previous incarnation, including a newly-designed straight-leg swing-arm frame, a huge 5 gallons (23 litre) 'turnpike' type fuel tank and ball-ended hand-levers. A 12V electrical system was fitted to provide sufficient power for starting the 1,213cc (74cu.in) engine. The increased size of the battery – rated at 32Ah – necessitated the use of a new-shaped rectangular oil tank fitted with internal filters. The starter was located behind the rearmost cylinder and engaged on the primary drive. Early examples were said to be temperamental in the wet, so it was as well that a kickstarter was also fitted. The cast aluminium primary chain covers were bolted directly to the transmission case for increased strength; a shoe being fitted inside the case to adjust the chain tension since it was no longer possible to slide back the primary covers.

Technical specification

Models XL, XLA, XLH 'Sportster'.

Engine:
883cc (53.9cu.in) Harley-Davidson '55'; two cylinders in 45° 'V' formation; bore and stroke, 2.99in x 3.8in (76mm x 97mm); overhead valves; air cooled; dry sump; power output, 42–58bhp at 6,800rpm; torque, 52lbf/ft at 3,500rpm. Larger engine fitted from 1972, but not used for military service in this form.

Transmission:
4 F; foot gear-change; multi-plate dry clutch (wet clutch from 1971); duplex primary roller-chain running in closed casing; exposed roller-chain drive to rear wheel; primary and secondary chains on right-hand side of motor.

Suspension:
coil spring suspension on front forks, swinging arm with coil springs at rear; hydraulic dampers.

Electrical system:
(1957 to 1964) 6V, (from 1965) 12V, battery.

Brakes:
mechanically operated drum brakes; front and rear.

Tyre size:
3.50-18, same size front and rear; from 1960, the XLCH was fitted with a 3.50-19 front tyre.

Construction:
cycle type steel-tube frame.

Dimensions
Length, 90in (2.3m); *width*, 35in (89cm); *height*, 40in (102cm). *Wheelbase*, 60.2in (1.53m). *Ground clearance*, 4.45in (113mm). *Unladen weight*, 465lb (211kg).

Performance
Maximum allowable speed, 93mph to 110mph (150kph to 177kph). Range of action, n/a. Average fuel consumption, n/a.

Comprehensive performance and dimensional data was not always available for militarised civilian models.

Although there was not a separately-designated sidecar model, the standard sidecar for use with this range was the old-faithful Model LE. Three-speed transmission with reverse was available for sidecar outfits.

Despite a price increase of $145 over the previous year, making the FLB $1,530 and the FLHB $1,595, sales were particularly buoyant with 6,930 machines sold in 1965.

The following year, 1966, the 'Panhead' engine was replaced by the more powerful 'Shovelhead' unit. This engine was fitted with aluminium 'Power-Pac' cylinder heads, new

Right: Examples of what was essentially a civilian Model FLHB 'Electra-Glide' were purchased by the Belgian Army's Rijkswacht in 1967. (DK)

Below: The hugely-successful 1,213cc (74cu.in) 'Electra-Glide' range was launched in 1965 with four models: total production over 17 years amounted to 128,120 units. The model was popular with law enforcement agencies, both military (as here) and civilian, and also has the distinction of being the last use of full-size Harley-Davidsons by a European army. (NA)

Technical specification

Models FLB, FLFB, FLHB, FLHFB 'Electra-Glide'.

Engine:
1,213cc (74cu.in) Harley-Davidson '74'; two cylinders in 45° 'V' formation; bore and stroke, 3.4in x 3.98in (87mm x 101mm); overhead valves; air cooled; dry sump; power output, 54–62bhp at 5,400rpm; torque, 62 lbf/ft at 3,200rpm. 1,311cc (80cu.in) engine offered as an option (Model FLH-80) from 1978 to 1980, and fitted as standard to all FLH models for 1981; not used by the military in this form.

Transmission:
4F or 3F1R (for sidecar outfits); hand or foot gear-change; multi-plate dry clutch, wet from 1968; triplex primary roller-chain running in closed casing; exposed roller-chain drive to rear wheel; primary chain on left-hand side of motor, secondary chain on right.

Suspension:
coil spring suspension on front forks, swinging arm with coil springs at rear; hydraulic dampers.

Brakes:
1965 to 1971, mechanically operated drum brakes, front and rear; 1972, hydraulic disc brake at front, drum at rear; from 1973, hydraulic disc brakes, front and rear.

Tyre size:
5.00-16, same size front and rear.

Construction:
duplex steel-tube frame.

Electrical system:
12V battery.

Dimensions
Length, 93in (2.4m); *width*, 35in (89cm); *height*, 31in (79cm).
Wheelbase, 61in (1.6m).
Ground clearance, 4.65in (118mm).
Unladen weight, 555lb (252kg).

Performance
Maximum allowable speed, 103mph (166kph).
Range of action, n/a.
Average fuel consumption, n/a.

Comprehensive performance and dimensional data was not always available for militarised civilian models.

design pushrods and a new air cleaner. The carburettor was changed from a Linkert to Tillotson late in the year, this resulted in a 10% increase in power. The new 'Shovelhead' engine was also said to be quieter and more oil-tight. Prices were increased to $1,545 for the Models FLB and FLFB and $1,610 for the higher-compression FLHB and FLFHB. Production for the year rose to 7,800 units.

Changes for 1967 amounted to little more than a revised rear brake drum, hubs and axles. Sales scarcely dipped at 7,750 for the year and the machines were priced at $1,735 and $1,800. Astonishingly, the Belgian Army's *Rijkswacht* purchased a small number of what was essentially a civilian Model FLHB 'Electra-Glide' in 1967.

By 1968, Harley-Davidson was facing a financial crisis and there was little money available to make any changes to the product; the only significant change was the adoption of a wet clutch with improved springs. The prices remained unchanged and sales for the year totalled 6,950 units.

Left: The last Harley-Davidsons to be used for Military Police work in the USA were Model XLAs from 1963. (NA)

Right: Despite falling military sales, the big Harley-Davidson remained a popular choice with law enforcement agencies. The actress Jayne Mansfield is handing out a speeding ticket in this publicity photograph. (NA)

Changes to the machines were also minimal in 1969, with little more than the front brake relocated from the left to the right, and fitted with a new operating cam. Improvements were also made to the wiring harness. However, 1969 was the year when the company agreed a take-over by the American Machine & Foundry Company (AMF). Sales appeared unaffected, with a total of 7,300 units for the year and at prices of $1,885 and $1,900.

The big improvement for 1970 was the replacement of the generator by an alternator and rectifier. Changes were also made to the timing gears, the timing case, the crankcase and the oil tank. The 'B' was dropped from the designation and the models were described as the FLH and FLHF, replacing the FLB and FLFB. The FLP and FLPF replaced the higher-performance models. As before the 'F' suffix in the code indicated foot-operated gear change. Production climbed to 7,615.

Again, little changed in 1971 but the carburettor was changed to a Bendix/Zenith type, operated by a standard twist-grip throttle. A total of 6,675 machines were sold.

A 10in (25.4cm) front disc brake was adopted in 1972 and 9,700 machines were sold. The rear brake was changed to a hydraulic disc the following year and the kick-starter was finally removed. The range was rationalised down to just two models, the FL and FLH, and the option of hand gear-change was finally deleted. Sales for 1973 amounted to 8,775.

The carburettor was changed again in 1974, this time to a Keihin type and the Model FLHF was reintroduced. A new low-compression model, the FLP, was offered, especially for police forces. Total sales of these models stood at 7,267 for the year. There were no significant changes for 1975 and sales amounted to 2,435.

For 1976, the range stood at just one model, now known as the FLH-1200 and, for 1977, this was joined by a limited edition, designated Model FLHS, essentially the same machine, albeit with different finish and accessories, designated Model FLHS. Both models were fitted with improved transmission. Sales reached 11,891 for 1976 and 9,226 for 1977.

Three models were offered for 1978: the FLH, FLH 'Anniversary' with special finish, and the FLH-80, which was fitted with a larger 1,311cc (80cu.in) engine and 'sported' elaborate cast wheels. Sales climbed again, to a total of 9,406.

There was a degree of rethinking for 1979 and the line-up featured five different models: the FLH-1200 was the standard solo machine with the 1,213cc (74cu.in) engine; the FLH-80 was fitted with the larger 1,311cc (80cu.in) engine and FLHCE was the sidecar equivalent; FLHP-1200 and FLHP-80 were police models; and the FLHC was the so-called 'classic' model with the 1,311cc (80cu.in) engine, special paint finish and cast wheels. A total of 11,442 units were sold.

The same line-up was offered for 1980 when all models were fitted with Motorola electronic ignition. Total sales for the year amounted to 6,598.

From 1981, the 1,213cc (74cu.in) engine was finally deleted and all of the models in the range were fitted with the 1,311cc (80cu.in) engine. In this form, and with the later 'Evolution' engine, the 'Electra-Glide' remained in production into the early years of the new millennium.

Total production of the 1,213cc (74cu.in) 'Electra-Glide' during the 17-year run amounted to 128,120 machines, making this a huge success for the company.

MODEL MT

There are those who perhaps might not consider the Model MT to be a 'proper' Harley-Davidson. It was, after all, derived from a road machine produced by the Italian SWM company in the early 1980s as the XN Tornado, before passing to the British company Armstrong-CCM of Bolton, Lancashire. It was not until 1987 that Harley-Davidson became involved, buying the rights to the model when Armstrong withdrew from the market. The company continued to manufacture the machine and to supply the British Army who had been buying from Armstrong. Harley-Davidson also attempted to sell the machine to other friendly nations. The original motorcycle, a nominal 500cc (30.6cu.in) trials type machine, had been developed by SWM to provide a street-legal model to sell alongside their competition machines; the company also manufactured a military variant. When SWM ran into financial difficulties, the rights to the model were sold to Armstrong-CCM who also had the UK rights to produce the Canadian-designed Can-Am Bombardier which was in use with UK and other NATO forces. The common thread between the motorcycles produced by SWM and Bombardier was that both were powered by a Rotax engine. This engine was manufactured in a factory at Gunskirchen, Wels, Austria which, at the time, was owned by Bombardier.

Armstrong claimed in sales literature that the MT500 had been specifically designed to meet the requirements of the British Ministry of Defence (MoD) according to the specification S785:1984. This suggests that it was rather more than an Anglicised version of the Tornado. Indeed, Armstrong had spent two years developing the design into a reliable military motorcycle, beating-off competition for the contract from 16 other manufacturers. In 1985 the company announced that they had won the contract to supply 2,300 machines to the MoD, where it was to replace the 250cc (15.3cu.in) Bombardier Can-Am.

Right: The Rotax-engined MT350 (shown) and the larger-engined MT500, which had been originally produced by the Armstrong-CCM, replaced the Bombardier in British Army service in 1985. Armstrong's motorcycle interest was sold to Harley-Davidson in October 1987 and the machines were rebadged. (MoD)

Despite an uncompromising off-road appearance, the machines were just as frequently used for normal despatch rider duties. It was said to be heavy on the road and not suitable for competitive cross-country work, but the MT500 was sturdy and reliable.

Powered by a Rotax four-valve single-cylinder engine of 485cc (29.6cu.in), key features of the MT500 included five-speed transmission, heavy-duty hydraulic suspension,

solid-state ignition system, sealed-for-life drive chain, water- and dust-resistant brakes. Aluminium wheel rims were fitted. World War Two-style canvas pannier bags were carried on side racks at the rear, each large enough to carry a Jerrycan. A substantial rear rack was also fitted. Although the MT500 was generally equipped with a kick starter – said to be difficult to start due to carburettor settings and the curious left-leg starter position – a number were also fitted with electric starter. The

Technical specification

Models MT500, M50, MT350E.

Engine:
(MT500 and MT50) 485cc (30cu. in), (MT350E) 348cc (21cu.in) Rotax; single cylinder; bore and stroke, 3.5in x 3.0in (89mm x 77mm), or 3.1in x 2.8in (80mm x 70mm), respectively; overhead valves, single over-head cam; air cooled; dry sump; power output, 33bhp at 6,200rpm, or 30bhp at 8,000rpm, respectively; torque, 28lbf/ft at 5,500rpm, or 20lbf/ft at 6,500rpm, respectively.

Transmission:
5 F; foot gear-change; gearbox unit-constructed with engine; multi-plate wet clutch; exposed sealed-for-life roller-chain drive to rear wheel with O-ring seals; drive chain on right-hand side of the engine.

Suspension:
Marzocchi sealed heavy-duty telescopic front forks with hydraulic damping; Ohlins trailing helical-spring rear, adjustable for load.

Brakes:
MT50, MT500, mechanically operated drum brakes, front and rear; MT350E, hydraulic disc brakes, front and rear.

Tyre size:
front, 90/90-21; rear, 4.00-18.

Construction:
cycle type steel-tube and box-section frame, incorporating integral oil reservoir.

Electrical system:
12V battery.

Dimensions
Length, 87in (2.2m); *width,* 31in (79cm); *height,* 46in (1.2m).
Wheelbase, 57in (1.45m).
Ground clearance, 8.5in (216mm).
Unladen weight, 330 to 355lbs (149.7 to 161kg).

Performance
Maximum allowable speed, 80 to 90mph (129 to 145kph), according to engine.
Range of action, 150 to 200 miles (241 to 322km).
Average fuel consumption, 50 to 60mpg (18 to 21kpl).

army of Jordan received 500 machines and the army of Canada were supplied with 100. The machine delivered to Canada was confusingly designated the M50.

The MT500 was the best known of the original machines, but Armstrong also offered 348cc (21.26cu.in) and 560cc (32.2cu.in) engines in what was substantially the same package, the former designated MT350.

In October 1987, the Armstrong company was sold to Harley-Davidson, who were already using Rotax engines in the machines produced for the company's dirt-track race team. It was said that the company were keen to supply motorcycles to NATO, but part of the reason for the purchase of Armstrong may also have been the fact that, in 1986, the US Army announced a plan to purchase 6,000 motorcycles. Sadly, the funding for this was never made available.

However, with a handful of detailed design changes, Harley-Davidson kept the MT500 in production, simply re-badging the machines to reflect the new ownership. Note that production of MT500s for Canada continued until the early 1990s, which means that many Canadian machines latterly wore the Harley-Davidson badge.

Right: The Armstrong-designed MT350 (shown here in prototype form) was first supplied to the Ministry of Defence during 1985; the smaller-engined MT350 followed in 1993 and both were also produced by Harley-Davidson after the company acquired Armstrong in 1987. (DC)

In 1993, the British MoD announced a further order for 1,570 of these motorcycles (contract number LV2A/067). The contract specified the smaller-engined MT350, with the addition of electric start, which changed the designation to MT350E. Some have suggested that the MT350E was substituted for the MT500 as a result of UK learner-driver licensing rules. The smaller-engined model was a logical development of the original machine, still using a Rotax engine, but now fitted with an improved carburettor and electric-starting. There were also new disc brakes at the front and rear. Visually, the canvas panniers were removed in favour of one-piece moulded plastic 'document boxes' with a waterproof hinged lid. In an attempt to conceal the thermal signature of the engine, these boxes were fitted to the frame down-tube where they obscured the engine. A gun box was often fitted to the right-hand rear fork.

The MT35E was manufactured at Harley-Davidson's plant at York, Pennsylvania at a rate of two machines a day.

Although Harley-Davidson manufactured both the MT500 and the MT350E, there was no suggestion that either of these machines would ever be sold in the civilian marketplace or be available through the company's dealers. Similarly, neither machine had been available to the civilian market when produced by Armstrong-CCM. The company did announce that the machine would be available under contract to other friendly governments and Harley-Davidson remained keen to interest the US Army. A number of MT500s were thought to have been used by USAF 'combat control teams' but, sadly, the US Army went on to buy the Kawasaki KL-250D8, which was $2,000 cheaper than the MT350E.

Total production of all MT models, by both Armstrong and Harley-Davidson during an almost 20-year production run, was 4,470 motorcycles.

HARLEY-DAVIDSON MILITARY MOTORCYCLES
Intended for US Army use unless otherwise indicated

Date	Model/ frame number prefix	Description	Engine and transmission: capacity		cyls	gears	Notes
1912	X-8-A	Motorcycle, solo	492cc	(30cu.in)	1	1	Japan
1916	16-J	Motorcycle, solo	999cc	(61cu.in)	V2	3	(and Denmark, trials only)
1916	16-J/LC	Motorcycle, with sidecar	999cc	(61cu.in)	V2	3	
1916	16-J/GC	Motorcycle, with machine-gun sidecar	999cc	(61cu.in)	V2	3	
1916	16-J/AC	Motorcycle, with ammunition sidecar	999cc	(61cu.in)	V2	3	
1916	16-J/SC	Motorcycle, with stretcher sidecar	999cc	(61cu.in)	V2	3	
1917	17-E	Motorcycle, solo	999cc	(61cu.in)	V2	1	
1917	17-J	Motorcycle, solo	999cc	(61cu.in)	V2	3	
1917	17-J/LC	Motorcycle, with sidecar	999cc	(61cu.in)	V2	3	
1917	17-J/P	Motorcycle, with sidecar	999cc	(61cu.in)	V2	3	Soviet Union
1918	18-E	Motorcycle, solo	999cc	(61cu.in)	V2	1	
1918	18-FUS	Motorcycle, solo	999cc	(61cu.in)	V2	3	
1918	18-J	Motorcycle, solo	999cc	(61cu.in)	V2	3	
1918	18-J/LC	Motorcycle, with sidecar	999cc	(61cu.in)	V2	3	
1919	19-FUS	Motorcycle, solo	999cc	(61cu.in)	V2	3	
1919	19-FUS/LUS	Motorcycle, with sidecar	999cc	(61cu.in)	V2	3	
1922	22-FS/LUS	Motorcycle, with sidecar	999cc	(61cu.in)	V2	3	
1923	(Rock Island Arsenal)	Power cart, 300 lb (136kg), tracked	574cc	(35cu.in)	H2	3	Prototype, HD engine only
1923	(Rock Island Arsenal)	Power cart, 450 lb (204kg), tracked	574cc	(35cu.in)	H2	3	Prototype, HD engine only
1924	(Rock Island Arsenal)	Power cart, 450 lb (204kg), 4x4; M1924	1,213cc	(74cu.in)	V2	3	Prototype, HD engine only
1924	(Rock Island Arsenal)	Power cart, 450 lb (204kg), 4x4; M1924E	999cc	(61cu.in)	V2	3	Prototype, HD engine only
1924	24-JD	Motorcycle, solo	1,213cc	(74cu.in)	V2		
1930	30-VL	Motorcycle, solo	1,213cc	(74cu.in)	V2	3	

Date	Model/ frame number prefix	Description	Engine and transmission: capacity	cyls	gears	Notes
1932	32-RL	Motorcycle, solo	737cc (45cu.in)	V2	3	
1932	32-VS/LT	Motorcycle, with sidecar	1,213cc (61cu.in)	V2	3	(and Denmark, trials only)
1932	32-VS/LC (Landsverk 210)	Motorcycle, with armoured sidecar	1,213cc (61cu.in)	V2	3	Denmark
1933	33-RL	Motorcycle, solo	737cc (45cu.in)	V2	3	
1933	33-VL/LT	Motorcycle, with sidecar	1,213cc (61cu.in)	V2	3	China
1934	34-RL	Motorcycle, solo	737cc (45cu.in)	V2	3	
1934	34-VDS/LT	Motorcycle, with sidecar	1,213cc (61cu.in)	V2	3	
1936	36-RL	Motorcycle, solo	737cc (45cu.in)	V2	3	
1937	37-WL	Motorcycle, solo	737cc (45cu.in)	V2	3	
1937	(Sankyo Rikuo 97)	Motorcycle, solo	737cc (45cu.in)	V2	3	Licence-built, Japan
1937	(Sankyo Rikuo 97)	Motorcycle, with sidecar	1,196cc (73cu.in)	V2	3	Licence-built, Japan
1939	39-ELA/LE	Motorcycle, with sidecar	999cc (61cu.in)	V2	4	
1939	39-U	Motorcycle, solo	1,213cc (74cu.in)	V2	4	
1939	39-UA	Motorcycle, solo	1,213cc (74cu.in)	V2	4	
1939	39-US/LE	Motorcycle, with sidecar	1,213cc (74cu.in)	V2	4	
1939	39-WL	Motorcycle, solo	737cc (45cu.in)	V2	3	(and Denmark, trials only)
1940	40-ELA/LLE	Motorcycle, with sidecar	999cc (61cu.in)	V2	4	
1940	40-TA	Motor tricycle, field car, 3x2	999cc (61cu.in)	V2	3	Experimental
1940	40-TA (modified)	Motor tricycle, field car, 3x2	1,130cc (69cu.in)	V2	3	Modified experimental
1940	40-WLA	Motorcycle, solo	737cc (45cu.in)	V2	3	
1941	41-ELA/LE	Motorcycle, with sidecar	999cc (61cu.in)	V2	4	
1941	41-ELC/LE	Motorcycle, with sidecar	999cc (61cu.in)	V2	4	Canada
1941	41-ELC/LLE	Motorcycle, with sidecar	999cc (61cu.in)	V2	4	Britain, ex-Canadian Army
1941	41-GA 'Servi-Car'	Motor tricycle, 3x2	737cc (45cu.in)	V2	3F1R	
1941	41-GA 'Servi-Car'	Motor tricycle, 3x2, with GE radio	737cc (45cu.in)	V2	3F1R	
1941	41-UH	Motorcycle, solo, with RCA radio	1,311cc (80cu.in)	V2	4	
1941	41-UA	Motorcycle, solo	1,213cc (74cu.in)	V2	4	
1941	41-WLA	Motorcycle, solo	737cc (45cu.in)	V2	3	
1941	41-WLC	Motorcycle, solo	737cc (45cu.in)	V2	3	Canada

Date	Model/ frame number prefix	Description	Engine and transmission: capacity		cyls	gears	Notes
1942	42-XA	Motorcycle, solo	739cc	(45cu.in)	H2	4	
1942	42-ELA/LE	Motorcycle, with sidecar	999cc	(61cu.in)	V2	4	
1942	42-ELC/LE	Motorcycle, with sidecar	999cc	(61cu.in)	V2	4	Canada
1942	42-US/LE	Motorcycle, with sidecar	1,213cc	(74cu.in)	V2	4	
1942	42-US/LLE	Motorcycle, with sidecar	1,213cc	(74cu.in)	V2	4	South Africa
1942	42-WLA	Motorcycle, solo	737cc	(45cu.in)	V2	3	
1942	42-WLA (modified)	Motorcycle, solo, 3x2	737cc	(45cu.in)	V2	3	Experimental, twin rear wheel
1942	42-WLC	Motorcycle, solo	737cc	(45cu.in)	V2	3	Canada
1942	42-WLS/LS	Motorcycle, with sidecar	737cc	(45cu.in)	V2	3	
1943	43-ELA/LE	Motorcycle, with sidecar	999cc	(61cu.in)	V2	4	
1943	43-US/LLE	Motorcycle, with sidecar	1,213cc	(74cu.in)	V2	4	South Africa
1943	42-WLA	Motorcycle, solo	737cc	(45cu.in)	V2	3	
1943	43-WLC	Motorcycle, solo	737cc	(45cu.in)	V2	3	Canada
1943	42-XA	Motorcycle, solo	739cc	(45.2cu.in)	H2	4	
1943	42-XAS	Motorcycle, with sidecar, 3x2	739cc	(45.2cu.in)	H2	4	
1943	(Willys WAC)	Truck, extra-lightweight, 4x4	802cc	(49cu.in)	H2	3	Prototypes, HD engine only
1944	44-ES/LE	Motorcycle, with sidecar	999cc	(61cu.in)	V2	4	
1944	44-FS/LE	Motorcycle, with sidecar	1,213cc	(74cu.in)	V2	4	
1944	44-US/LE	Motorcycle, with sidecar	1,213cc	(74cu.in)	V2	4	
1944	42-WLA	Motorcycle, solo	737cc	(45cu.in)	V2	3	
1944	43-WLC	Motorcycle, solo	737cc	(45cu.in)	V2	3	Canada
1944	(Willys WAC-3)	Truck, platform, 4x4	802cc	(49cu.in)	H2	3	Prototype, HD engine only
1945	45-WL	Motorcycle, solo	737cc	(45cu.in)	V2	3	
1945	42-WLA	Motorcycle, solo	737cc	(45cu.in)	V2	3	
1945	45-WLR	Motorcycle, solo	737cc	(45cu.in)	V2	3	Soviet Union
1945	45-WSR/LS	Motorcycle, with sidecar, 3x2	737cc	(45cu.in)	V2	3	Prototype, Soviet Union
1948	48-S	Motorcycle, light, solo	123cc	(7.5cu.in)	1	3	Military trials only
1949	49-WLA	Motor cycle, solo	737cc	(45cu.in)	V2	3	
1950	50-G 'Servi-Car'	Motor tricycle, 3x2	737cc	(45cu.in)	V2	3F1R	

Date	Model/ frame number prefix	Description	Engine and transmission: capacity		cyls	gears	Notes
1950	50-WLA	Motorcycle, solo	737cc	(45cu.in)	V2	3	
1951	51-WLA	Motorcycle, solo	737cc	(45cu.in)	V2	3	
1952	52-WLA	Motorcycle, solo	737cc	(45cu.in)	V2	3	
1953	53-KA	Motorcycle, solo	737cc	(45cu.in)	V2	4	
1956	56-KH 'Sport'	Motorcycle, solo	901cc	(55cu.in)	V2	4	Netherlands
1963	63-XLA 'Sportster'	Motorcycle, solo	901cc	(55cu.in)	V2	4	
1967	67-FLH 'Electra-glide'	Motorcycle, solo	1,213cc	(74cu.in)	V2	4	Belgium
1987	M50	Motorcycle, solo	485cc	(30cu.in)	1	4	Canada, Jordan
1987	MT500	Motorcycle, solo	485cc	(30cu.in)	1	4	Britain
1990	MT500	Motorcycle, solo	485cc	(30cu.in)	1	4	
1993	MT350E	Motorcycle, solo	349cc	(21cu.in)	1	4	Britain